The Saving Seed

Growing a Financially Healthy Family Tree

By Ashley Parks, CFP®

ISBN-10: 0615494358

EAN-13: 9780615494357

Table of Contents

A Note to the Reader

I dedicate this book to my daughter Madison and to all the other amazing children who hold the light of this world in their hearts. I give gratitude to my Creator, my family and friends who have given me strength and courage to grow beyond myself.

Forward

From as early as I can remember, I've had a feeling deep within of the true person that I am at my core. It's that seed that was planted the day I came into being, the day I was born and began to grow. Over time, experiences and lessons we learn from those experiences shape the person we become. Some of those experiences are positive and have helped us grow. Some are like weeds that seep into our inner being and try to change who we are at the core.

When asked why and how I wrote the book **The Saving Seed: Growing a Financially Healthy Family Tree**, I thought "I have to do this, I have something important to share with the world and I have to think bigger than myself. It's time for me to grow again." I've been practicing financial planning for over 12 years and have started to see financial patterns in people. Financial roots lead people to make financial decisions, to see the

world from a formed perspective and to continue those patterns in adult-hood. People shared their stories with me. Their experiences affected who they grew up to be and were affecting their financial behaviors. We were uncovering the "why" of their current financial behaviors. It's as if in an instant people were brought back in time to when they saw the world, including the financial world, the way they did. Change doesn't occur by mere recognition of ourselves; rather change occurs when we act on what we've learned. A decision to change has no effect without action.

In my own spiritual journey, I've uncovered that in order to find that core again, we must reclaim our ground. We must pull up our sleeves and dig in the dirt, prune, pull weeds and learn how to nourish ourselves and our surroundings so that we can be healthy. This book helps us to work through our root system to find that healthy seed again. I walk the reader through the process of clearing out our gardens and how to grow healthy seeds for the next generation.

As in life, we don't reach one level and simply stay there. We either move forward or backward. We grow or we lose part of ourselves. I want to encourage people to be strong and to do what is necessary for true inner growth to occur. In strengthening our core, our root system, we start to see healthy fruits come into our lives. On a daily basis, we must be conscious of the habits needed to maintain that health, whether spiritually, physically, mentally or financially. Wouldn't it be wonderful if we could model those behaviors for our children? I wrote The Saving Seed as a tool to help you do just that.

The Saving Seed

T he seeds we plant in our children, as the seeds that were planted in us, shape who they are and who they grow up to be. Those seeds determine the strength and character of the root system that develops. The financial seeds we plant determine what our family money tree will look like. What seeds are you planting? Is your family money tree healthy and strong? This book will help you to understand what seeds to plant, determine what kind of roots *you* have and how to grow a financially healthy family money tree.

Imagine children growing up feeling comfortable with financial decisions, understanding budgeting, saving and giving to charity. Imagine your college-aged child educated to make good choices about expenses, credit and debt. Imagine your child entering the work force with knowledge about retirement strategies, investments and life planning. Understanding

1

money in your family is crucial not only to your *child's* survival, but a healthy relationship with money is what is needed for our *country* to survive. The messages we send, whether explicit or implicit, bear weight on how your children will view money for the rest of their lives. Plant good seeds and become a part of changing our future financial landscape.

I contemplate the parable in Luke 8:5-8 *(NIV)*. "A farmer went out to sow his seed. As he was scattering the seed, some fell along the path; it was trampled on, and the birds ate it up. Some fell on rocky ground, and when it came up, the plants withered because they had no moisture. Other seed fell among thorns, which grew up with it and chocked the plants. Still other seed fell on good soil. It came up and yielded a crop, a hundred times more than was sown." We cannot merely throw seeds out and hope growth will occur. We must cultivate the soil, lay the groundwork, for the seeds we scatter to take root.

The day we find out we're going to be parents marks a new chapter in our lives. Maybe you don't have kids, but you're the best aunt, uncle, friend or mentor a child could have. When you call yourself Mom, Dad, Aunt, Uncle, Friend or Mentor, you take responsibility for helping those who come after you. Not only do we have the responsibility to nourish, protect and encourage our children, but we also have to set the example for them. Did I lose anyone already?

We have to set the example ourselves. The phrase "do as I say, not as I do" just doesn't cut it today and really never worked long-term. A parent telling a child never to smoke cigarettes, but who smokes daily in front of the child sends a mixed message, "Why is it so bad if Mom or Dad does it?" You are probably thinking back in your life and nodding your head in agreement. I grew up in a generation where candy cigarettes were the candy of choice. You could even blow fake candy smoke out of them. You could get on an airplane and specify the smoking or non-smoking section for seating. Airlines would even offer cigarettes to their passengers like

they do with peanuts today. Times have changed and research has shown how harmful smoking is and we've had to change the way we view certain habits. We don't have an excuse anymore because we know better. It's our willingness to learn and adapt and model healthy habits for our kids that takes effort and commitment.

Actions do speak louder than words, and we need to show, not tell, our children how to be good stewards of their money. As adults, we are faced with so many responsibilities that adding even one more task can seem too difficult to manage. As parents or guardians, it might seem like just getting through the day is enough. It is understandable to think, "Everyone made it home in one piece, we were fed, clothed, and we can now rest our weary heads for another night." But this does not guide a child to a better financial life. Guiding a child to a better financial life does not necessarily mean giving the next generation a better standard of living; rather, it means imparting it with a better understanding of money—how money pervades every part of life and a greater sense of financial responsibility. We come from all walks of life. Whether you live in a 20,000 square-foot home or a 500 square-foot apartment, the principles are the same. Developing a strong financial root system will be the foundation of a strong and healthy money tree.

In reading this book, I want you to be able to equip yourself with the knowledge and motivation needed to truly impact the next group of kids that comes along. In doing so, you have to work on yourself. You will lose credibility if you don't practice what you preach. What we do crystallizes the habits—both good and bad—that will accompany your children into adulthood. How can we teach them about things that we ourselves may struggle with? The answer is that we must educate ourselves. We must develop good habits and train ourselves to persevere and to be resilient. We must show them what it looks like to lead a financially responsible household. We talk about money with them in an age-appropriate way so that

this topic never becomes taboo. We must teach them to respect what they have rather than feeling entitled. Isn't that what we'd want for our children? I know I do, and almost every other parent with whom I've talked agrees.

You may be saying to yourself, "Great, I thought this book was about what to tell our kids." It is. But there is a difference between hearing and understanding. Only by setting the example will they actually understand it. I've worked with many families over the years to help them along the path toward a solid financial foundation. But before ever getting started, we need to discover how people view money, where they learned their money habits and what conscious and subconscious beliefs they have about it. This is where the fun part begins.

Dr. Ted Klontz is a financial therapist and author of *Mind Over Money: Overcoming the Money Disorders That Threaten Our Financial Health* (Klontz). In an interview with Dr. Klontz, he describes financial health as existing "when an individual's experience includes low levels of financial stress, absence of self-defeating financial behaviors, and a comprehensive awareness of their financial condition all of which help create a basic overall senses of financial peace and security." (Kontz) Financial health does not mean abundance. Some could argue that if they only had more money that all or most of their problems would go away. Wrong. Financial health refers to the state of your financial affairs, such as how much debt you have compared to your assets, your cash flow management and savings levels.

I asked Dr. Klontz what consequences, in his experience, does leading an unhealthy financial life have on a person? "High levels of stress (in study after study money is the number one stressor for all Americans) and (since money is one of those things in our lives that touches, in some way, every aspect of our lives) a lower quality and enjoyment of life." He goes on to say that "at least 90% of all our behaviors are generated by our unconscious mind. Early childhood experiences 'program' this unconscious mind and are the source of subsequent behaviors. Consider something as innocent as being exposed to the children's song, 'Hush Little Baby.' If you listen to the message of the song, happiness can be found if you just purchase (or are given) the right thing, and if you aren't happy, you just haven't purchased (or been given) the right thing yet. In other words, 'Money makes you happy.' That message is what we mean by a money script. Another example is a child who witnesses her grandmother coming in at the last moment and financially rescuing her son and his family (of which the child is a part) from foreclosure. Since money is one of those huge taboos and it is very unlikely that anyone will sit down with the child and explain that there won't always be a grandmother to the rescue, the child walks away believing 'the money will always be there.' That belief is an example of a money script. The beliefs are forgotten by our conscious mind, go to our unconscious mind and unknowingly drive future adult financial decision making." What are your roots? According to Dr. Ted Klontz, "all financial behaviors make sense if you understand the money scripts that drive them. All money scripts are based on some kind of experience that we have tried to understand, and quite often those scripts, taken as absolutes, are only partially true in some situations."

Each person has their own unique experiences. Even multiple people in the same household may handle the same circumstance very differently. This happens quite often with siblings who experienced a financial difficulty during childhood. One child became the hoarder, afraid of losing money and latching onto material items. The other child either couldn't face it or just threw her hands up, exclaimed "Who cares!" and entered adulthood with reckless abandon.

If you're blessed with more than one child, be sure to have family talks about money so that everyone hears the same information, and also make a point to spend some time alone with each child to talk about it. It's important that they are being heard, and that their individual fears or thoughts

are acknowledged. If there has been a financial change or challenge, be open and talk about it both as a family and with each child individually. One child may process change differently or think differently than another child. Maybe you have one right-brained child and one who is left-brained. Meet your child on his or her level so that working through issues is relevant to them.

Money discussions have been around for ages. According to *Crown Financial Ministries*™, there are 2,350 verses in the Bible relating to money, property and related matters. Contrary to popular belief, parents *should* be and need to be talking to their children about money. It's important on so many levels. Your little baby will be all grown up one day and will have to make financial decisions. You need to talk to your children—as well as show them what to do to manage their money. Your young adult needs to understand where money comes from and how it's spent, saved and invested by the time they leave your house. For the last 18 years, that child has relied on you for all the basic needs and for most of their wants. Then what? Push him into the real world without any idea of the financial and banking systems? If their school does have a curriculum on money, then this is a great opportunity for you and your child to begin an ongoing dialogue about it.

Discussing money in a level-headed, pragmatic manner is so important. Marriages can cease to exist from lack of communication about money. Show them what it looks like to have a clear, thoughtful discussion about money. Your children may remember that discussion when the time comes during their own adult relationships, and that memory should guide them well.

Getting Back to Your Roots

To better understand your roots, where you are and how you got here, I'd like to take a stroll back in history. In which economic environment were you raised? Are you a child of the Great Depression/the Silent Generation/the Traditionalist Generation? Are you a Baby Boomer? GenerationXer? GenerationYer/Millenial Generation? Each generation is a product of its own place in history. Each has taken a snapshot of the world and that picture has shaped their views and beliefs.

My grandfather lived during the Great Depression, which lasted from 1929 to 1939. If you are like him, you saw the world change drastically. Adults during that time were acutely aware of their assets evaporating seemingly overnight. October 24, 1929, dubbed "Black Thursday", marked the

beginning of the stock market collapse. Between 1933 and 1934, The Dow Jones Industrial Average, a widely used indicator of the condition of the stock market, lost 89 percent of its value. Roughly 25 percent of the total workforce was unemployed and looking for a job. According to the Federal Deposit Insurance Corporation, approximately 4,000 commercial banks and 1,700 Savings and Loans failed in 1933 (Planning).

To make matters worse, The Dust Bowl, a prolonged drought during the 1930s that resulted in an exodus of 3 million people from their farms in the Great Plains, further compounded the problem. During these tough times, people lost their homes, ate in soup kitchens and were on food rationing. In a letter my grandfather wrote describing that time, he mentioned rationing for household items like flour and sugar. Many households started home gardens to grow their own crops in their backyards both to save money and to have food available for their families.

The Great Depression left an indelible impact on people, and the result was a generation of individuals who were frugal, distrustful of the stock market and who were true savers. They learned how to stretch a dollar and to make thoughtful choices about where they spent their money. If you are the child of a Depression-era adult, the lessons your parents passed on most likely fell along those lines.

The Traditionalist Generation was born between 1927 and 1945. Traditionalists' parents came from the turn of the century. Their parents were hard workers; thus, their children saw work as a privilege. These children were taught to work hard and to earn their way, even if that meant working long hours and weekends, to get the job done. Higher education was often inaccessible for many Traditionalists.

The GI Bill of Rights, also known as the Servicemen's Readjustment Act, was signed into law by President Franklin D. Roosevelt on June 22, 1944. The GI Bill established a scholarship program for those who had served in uniform. By 1947, veterans accounted for 49 percent of college applicants. "By the time the original GI Bill ended on July 25, 1956, 7.8 million of the 16 million World War II veterans had participated in an education or training program," according to the United States Department of Veterans Affairs (Affairs). The GI Bill also set forth a provision for loans for homes, farms and businesses for veterans. From 1944 to 1952, Veterans Affairs backed roughly 2.4 million home loans for war veterans. This generation was educating itself, investing in businesses and becoming homeowners. Children of this generation may have had entrepreneurial parents who demonstrated hard work and owned businesses.

The Baby Boomers were born between 1946 and 1964. As the name suggests, the term describes the population boom resulting from the return of veterans from the European and Pacific theaters. With the addition of roughly 76 million babies (Bureau), the demand for consumer products, transportation and manufacturing soared. More schools had to be built to accommodate the surge of children. Shopping developments and businesses continued to grow to supply this new demand for products and services. Consumerism was in full force. In 1960, RCA had its Color TV launch with the campaign, "There's no TV like Color TV." You could now watch "The Price is Right" in full color and be exposed to novel and wonderful home appliances. This generation also was greatly impacted by reform and change in the 1960s. They were a part of the Civil Rights Movement, Woodstock, and the Vietnam War. Great figures of history such as Martin Luther King, Jr., the Kennedys and Lyndon B. Johnson lived at this time as well.

President Johnson signed the Civil Rights Act in 1964, which barred private employers from discriminating on the basis of sex, race, religion or national origin. Title VII created the Equal Employment Opportunity Commission (EEOC), an independent regulatory body, to implement the law. Baby boomers valued independence, free speech and the ability

to challenge authority, and there was media to broadcast it all across the globe. Employers could no longer discriminate, thus allowing a diverse work force to emerge. In 1950, labor force participation for women was 33.9 percent and the average family income was $4,237 (U. B. Statistics). Median household income in 1980 was $44,059 and $50,303 in 2008 (Bureau). In May 2011, women accounted for approximately 43 percent of full-time employed persons and accounted for 64 percent of part-time workers. (Statistics, 2011)

In 1963, although the Equal Pay Act established equal pay for men and women performing the same job duties, true equality in the workplace did not occur until much later. My mother, however, was an airline stewardess and there was a "no marriage" rule in the airline industry. My mother left her career to marry and start her family. *Sprogis v. United Air Lines, Inc.*, 517F.2d 387 (7th Cir. 1975), began the challenge to the airline no-marriage rule and was deemed illegal under Title VII of the Civil Rights Act of 1964. It wasn't until 1978 that Congress passed the Pregnancy Discrimination Act as an amendment to Title VII of the Civil Rights Act of 1964, which clarified that "Discrimination on the basis of pregnancy, childbirth or related medical conditions constitutes unlawful sex discrimination." I think of how far we've come. Women started working more and are better able to provide an income for themselves and their children.

Generation Xers, to which group I proudly belong, were born between 1965 and 1980. This generation typically grew up in a two-income household, thus earning the title "latch-key kid," meaning we let ourselves in at home after school since both parents were still at work. We saw both parents working, imbuing us with work ethic and responsibility. I can attest to this. My mother returned to work when my sister and I were in elementary school. Since both parents worked, I understood the need to share responsibilities around the house. I cleaned my room and helped with dinner when I was asked. When I grew older and needed to work a long day or even work on the weekend, it didn't really faze me since I saw my parents do the same and understood that everyone pitches in. Part of being in a family is doing your part. I have that motto today in my own family. We all have stuff—our clothes need to be washed, dishes put up and belongings put back. Personal awareness develops from responsibility.

I remember my father coming home from work, and taking the time to talk to me about his day and asking me about mine. I learned that even though you may have had a long day, you can always take the time to sit down with your child and talk. I value that time over any gift I was given or trip we ever took. As a mother, I can appreciate my mother having worked a full day yet taking time to cook a healthy meal for our family. The sacrifices we make and the seeds we plant do take root and will affect who your children become.

Generation X was the first generation to grow up with technology: computers, cell phones and the Internet. We were the "You've got mail" generation. I remember some of the first cell phones. They were about the size of a shoe box and plugged into your car. My father's office had a computer that took up an entire room. We've seen the 8-track player, the cassette tape, the compact disc and now most music is downloaded onto a device smaller than the palm of your hand. In college, we had to go to the library to use microfiche to look up historical stock prices in old newspapers. I can tell you with certainty that the Internet surely has made research easier.

Your age during this period may have affected how you viewed money. Early on, there was a sense of abundance and work. Interest rates in the 1980's were in the high teens. Paying an 18% mortgage rate on a 30-year mortgage was the norm. Later in the 1980s, the economy cycled into a recession, causing wealth to diminish and jobs to dissipate. I was old enough during this time to really see how that affected my community. That is actually the time when I decided I wanted to go into financial

planning. I saw how families in the 1980s went from good-sized homes to larger homes, mortgages increased and people wanted the new gadgets—those cell phones that were the size of a shoe box. When the economy turned southward, we downgraded which caused major stress in both our family and many of the families around us. I remember my parents saying, "I wish we would have just stayed in our first house…by now it would have been paid off." I see that today, with foreclosure signs posted outside many homes in our neighborhood. It's not the modest homes being foreclosed upon as much as the larger homes. Not only do they have a much higher mortgage payment, but the upkeep on those homes is high. You have to heat, cool, water and maintain much larger areas. Many people just couldn't keep such homes up. Anytime I get antsy to 'trade up,' I think about what we are blessed with. We have a nice home that we can afford and maintain. To me, that's peace of mind.

Generation Y came next. This group was born between 1981 and 2001. Some in this generation never knew life without cell phones, the Internet, and cable television. Many of them had parents that were Baby Boomers. Generation Yers view technology as a necessity. Imagine how much technology has changed our lives, both for the better and for the worse. From a positive standpoint, people can work remotely, multi-task and be up to speed on the news, world events and the markets. I can update my calendar, add my husband as an attendee, and have Microsoft Outlook remind him of certain appointments instead of me.

Edward M. Hallowell, MD, in his book *Crazy Busy* (Hallowell), defines new words that comically describe some of the new ways we cope with our busy lives. *Screensucking* is wasting time engaging with any screen. Think computer, flatscreen TV., iPad, and phone. There is also the *information addict* and the person that forgets due to *data overload*. Technology can be beneficial, but it can also do much harm.

Do this experiment with me: Total up the monthly and annual cost of your cable television, Internet, data plans and cell phones. Most of us wouldn't live without these items, correct? On the low end, people spend approximately $3,600 per year for these services, not including the cost to purchase the equipment which can run in the hundreds, if not thousands of dollars, and are out of date within a couple of years. I see people lament about their inability to save for retirement or establish basic savings, yet they are spending at the very minimum $300 per month on cable/Internet/data plan/cell phones.

Whichever generation you or your parents come from, there is a very important lesson to be learned. There were good times and bad in each era, and there will be good times and bad times again. The question is this: How are you going to handle them? What teachable moments can you share with others? How can we improve, despite hardships, and how can we be responsible when times are green again? I have heard wonderful stories from people about how their mother sewed their clothes, grew food and pickled produce for the pantry. I have also heard stories about parents who worked multiple jobs to provide for their families. The stories I heard were positive stories of family pride and of how their parents loved and provided for them. Even though they never had much, they never wanted much either. Consider the story of my father who always took the time to talk, and better yet, listen to his daughter.

My Roots

I was the kid who liked a challenge and always felt comfortable with money. Math was my strongest subject and I had a fairly decent dose of pragmatism. I also had great parents. One of my favorite money memories as a child involved rolling money. My dad had a wooden chest where he emptied his loose change everyday into the drawers. Over time the drawers became full and pretty heavy. One weekend, my mother was fed up with the money drawer and said that if I rolled my father's change and exchanged it at the bank, I could keep the money. I eagerly agreed. It seemed like I rolled for hours (by the way, this was in the days before Coinstar®). What didn't look like much more than loose change in a drawer amounted to over $100 in earnings for the day. I remember my dad finding out about the deal I had struck with my mother, unaware of the value of his little cash stash in the drawer. He wasn't thrilled to depart with the money, but he let me keep it for all the hard work and time I spent rolling all that change.

What my dad had also taught me was when you do business, you stick to the deal. I added about $100 to my savings that day.

My savings added up over time, bit by bit. I also made another choice: to save the money until a later date, for something bigger. Don't we want to teach our children to get work, do the work, get paid and save some or all of it? Over time, good work ethic develops, and with it comes valuing money. Before graduating college, I had waited tables, happily accepting the holiday hours when none of the others wanted to work, in order to get the big tips. I worked in retail and took advantage of the discounts for my clothes, sometimes up to 50 percent off. I was a chef at a bakery, and I brought home freshly baked goods that otherwise would have been thrown out that evening. I helped neighbors with errands, and I babysat and nannied, which was excellent practice for when I had my own child later in life.

All those experiences certainly afforded me great savings opportunities and tremendous exposure to all aspects of the work force. One hundred bucks here and another fifty there started adding up. I was able to pay for part of my first car and invested $4,000 while in college, which grew to $6,000 by the time I graduated. It was the 1990s, and I made my 50 percent fairly quickly and cashed out. I had $6,000 of my own money after college to get started, and no student loan debt thanks to my parents. I knew I wanted to be a Certified Financial Planner™ professional in college.

After graduation I took a job as a financial analyst in a corporation because it paid the most and I wanted to experience corporate life. If you've seen the movie, Office Space, you have a pretty good idea of what my corporate experience entailed. I was on my own and ready to face the world head on. I was suckered into the apartment deal. You get out of school, get a job and visit awesome apartments with the skyline view and the promise of nightlife within walking distance. What could be better? You justify the price difference between these and other places due to the amenities and

lifestyle. All of a sudden, you're paying for cable, a cell phone, gas card, and bills, bills, bills! I had fun for the year, but then found a great place that was $450 per month less and still had a fun atmosphere. I was getting paid a bit more than I was letting myself spend, and I was stashing the rest in savings for my escape from corporate life. I wanted to follow my dream, and I knew I'd need some savings to go after it.

A year and a half into my corporate job, I had enough saved and went for my dream. I'm writing this book more than 11 years later, living my dream and doing what I love. I truly believe that savings allowed me to do that. These are the same discussions I'm having with clients. What would you do if you could afford to do it?

What Seeds Were Planted in You?

We need to uncover what our beliefs, our assumptions, are because beliefs can be roadblocks on your financial and spiritual journey. Good seeds, properly cared for, grow healthy trees. Irrational or unhealthy beliefs are like weeds that can suck energy from the roots and stunt growth.

As adults, we have to open up some closets that maybe we've locked for years, decades even. What are your beliefs that you need to hang onto, and what needs to be dug up and thrown away? You may not even realize what some of them are. I like to use the analogy of taking a picture with your camera. We see the world through a set of lenses. The way we were raised, community and social influences, and personal experiences shape and color those lenses over time.

Imagine for a moment you have a camera. It is focused on a single object, so the other images surrounding are blurred. You're missing the

entire picture because you're just focused on one thing. We may then come to a conclusion based on seeing that one object of what the picture is about. Now change the focus so that the entire image is in view. What's new and different about the picture? Maybe you have a different perspective on what's happening in the scene. Finally, let's imagine you're using a wide-angle lens. There were objects that you couldn't even see before that had always been just beyond the periphery. Our beliefs may have us focusing in on one object in the big picture, whereas if we just widened our view, we'd see something very different. What I'm challenging you to do is to change out the lenses and widen your scope to look at your life from another perspective.

Michael Losier, author of *Law of Attraction*, used a great example of how to determine what our beliefs are. He refers to limiting beliefs. "They are usually found after you say the word because, as in the phrase, 'I can't because....'" (Losier 81) "I'm this way because everyone in my family is this way." That's a belief.

Take some time to address these questions. Write down your first reaction and what emotion you feel when answering them.

- ❧ What was your perception of money when you were young?
- ❧ What was the family dynamic (single parent raised you, Mom stayed at home, divorced parents, siblings, both parents worked)?
- ❧ How did that dynamic affect how money was spent and saved in your family?
- ❧ What money tensions were experienced in your family?
- ❧ Did something happen that made a lasting impact on how you view money?
- ❧ What was it, and how did it change you?
- ❧ When were you self-sufficient, and how did you handle it?

Next, take a break for a day or two and go back and read your answers. Do you still agree? Has time to think about your responses made you feel differently? You probably find that lessons learned from parents, community, peers and experiences and your emotional responses to those influences at a very early age are at the core of how you view money today. Seeds were planted and took root. You can't truly move forward until you discover your inner self and money motives and rewire your mind to think of the world differently than maybe you have done in the past. If you don't, you may temporarily improve, but your beliefs will try to pull you back into your old habits that threaten to derail you. I think about times in my garden when I've pulled weeds all afternoon, only to find them return shortly thereafter. The reality is that I pulled the leafy part off the weed, but was too lazy to dig up the roots. Those roots sprouted new weeds with the next rain. You've got to dig deep and get to the bottom of your beliefs.

What stories do you tell yourself about an experience? That inner dialogue is helpful in alerting us to what our beliefs are. I asked Dr. Ted Klontz about triggers which lead to our actions. Klontz says, "There are things in life that can stress us. When stress reaches a critical level, people seek relief from it. Some people drink, some people use money. 'Retail therapy' is not just a cute term. For some people, they have learned that shopping makes them feel better. For some people, money is a way to feel less lonely, less angry, less psychic pain (distraction). In other words, money is used as an attempt to meet emotional needs. It doesn't work long term. Money can't do that in the long term."

You need to know what happened so you can identify not only past triggers, but also what potential triggers may be. By identifying our thoughts and writing them down, we can see how our brain is working and determine whether those thoughts are in line with reality or not. What was your gut reaction to that thought and what did you do about it? Learn

healthy and realistic ways to handle the situation so that you're decisions and actions keep you on track with your goals.

Here's a personal anecdote. I really enjoy talking with people about money and giving financial presentations to groups. Every time I am about to speak, I feel a slight queasiness in my stomach and I am nervous. Let me repeat: I enjoy it, but it makes me feel unsettled. Why? A false belief that I have had in my life is that people don't want to learn about financial matters and that nobody is going to enjoy the presentation. There are some presenters that say they're giving an educational talk only to give the sales pitch at the end. I was afraid that when I spoke, people would be expecting to be sold something. However, I realized that the audience more than likely wouldn't be in attendance if that were the case.

The reality is that the people attending are there for the specific purpose of learning about money. I've trained myself to recognize why I have an emotional reaction, and I've also trained myself to silence that inner voice telling me nobody wants to hear about financial matters. After an initial deep breath, I start my presentation and really enjoy the talk, gain energy from it and feel good about further educating people on a topic I am passionate about. If I had listened to the initial voice originating from my false belief, I never would have spoken to groups about money management and certainly wouldn't be writing this book.

I'd like to focus on financial beliefs in this book but also challenge you to address other beliefs. What stories do you tell yourself? I've heard people who have struggled with alcohol say that people won't like them if they don't drink. Being disliked causes discomfort, so the person drinks alcohol. Needing alcohol to be liked is a false belief. People, in general, don't like or dislike someone based on what beverage they consume. These assumptions about how other people will react, how the situation will play out and how it will affect you may be 100 percent off base, but yet they hold you back from growing as a person.

Another false belief is thinking that people are thin because it's in their genes. The reality is that it may be a daily effort to exercise and make healthy eating choices to keep the weight off. When I've lost weight, I've thought, *"I can eat that, I'm thin."* Not so fast. That mentality is the root of why my weight has fluctuated in the past. If I eat everything I want, the weight will come back on.

I once heard a speaker use a great example regarding relationships and personal issues, but it could easily be used to describe financial matters. There is the fruit and then the tree. The fruit is really just an example of what the tree produces. You are the tree. The fruit could be your assets, liabilities, financial "issues" or the financial dynamic of your relationship with yourself, your spouse and your children. Do you have good fruit? In other words, do you have a good relationship with money? Are you living within your means? Do you have your assets and liabilities where they need to be? Are there financial stresses in your life? Healthy trees produce healthy fruit. If the fruit isn't good, you need to look to heal the tree because until you do, it won't produce good fruit.

Until you look at yourself and heal, you won't produce positive results and won't be able to plant good, healthy seeds in your family. Use this analogy with someone who is obese. Externally, we see extra pounds, medical issues and stress on the body. Would a truly healthy person have those issues? We can look at eating habits, exercise and medical history to gain some clues into what's causing these results, but the challenge is digging deeper. A fad diet won't heal the person. For long lasting change to improve the lifelong health of the person, we need to find out what that person's beliefs are about this issue. Is it a belief that changing eating habits doesn't work? Is it that the person believes he can't change? Is the person eating as a reaction to emotional stress? Does the person feel that everyone in his family is obese so he is destined to be also? Internal healing will manifest itself to create visible change.

Are you spending more than you make? Why? Do you make unhealthy financial decisions? Why? We all need a good pruning every now and then in order to get future growth. Get to the bottom of why and how you make your financial decisions, and seek the help needed to find the best path to get you on track. Your advisory team may consist of a good therapist, financial planner, accountant or religious or spiritual leader.

Take a look at the following phrases. Do any of these ring true if you're being *honest* with yourself?

- "I didn't have money growing up, so to feel fulfilled now, I spend… whether I have money or not."
- "I get a rush out of spending money. Even if I have to return the item I purchased, I still shop for the rush."
- "I had money growing up in my family, so I'm used to a certain life-style and I'm not willing to alter it."
- "When I was married and we had two incomes, I could afford what I wanted. My family is used to this lifestyle, and I like it and don't want myself or my kids to settle for less."
- "I work hard, so I feel that I deserve certain things, whether I have the money to pay for them or not."
- "It's important for me to appear successful to others, so I use my house, car and possessions as status symbols, even if I don't have the money to pay for them."
- "I feel guilty for my work schedule, so I buy things for my family, even when we don't have the money."
- "The breadwinner should make the financial decisions for the family. If you don't work, you don't get to decide where the money goes."
- "We don't talk about money in our family."
- "When times are hard I want to make myself happy, so I buy things to try to fulfill myself."

Ouch! What hit home for you? Find what struck you and face it head on. If you don't, your children will inherit your financial woes and be stuck with cleaning up your mess. And back to the tree example, you'll begin seeing some pretty rotten fruit dangling from your limbs. In tackling financial issues and decisions, it's important to face how you view money and how it influences your life. Changing how you view money can help to change your habits and help you to build a strong root system for financial success. Otherwise, your children will mimic your irresponsible behavior and the cycle will continue. The power is in your hands.

In the book *Born To Win* (Muriel and Jongeward 43) by Muriel James, Ph.D and Dorothy Jongeward, the authors explore the life plan that individuals follow. "Modern people wear many masks and have many forms of armor that keep their reality confined and unknown, even to themselves. The possibility of encountering one's own reality—learning about one's self—can be frightening and frustrating. Many people expect to discover the worst. A hidden fear lies in the fact that they may also discover the best. To discover the worst is to face the decision of whether or not to continue the same patterns. To learn the best is to face the decision of whether or not to live up to it. Either discovery may involve change and is therefore anxiety-provoking. However, this can be a creative anxiety which may be thought of as excitement—the excitement of enhancing one's possibilities for being a winner."

We moved into our house about ten years ago. There was a Bradford Pear tree in the back yard that I was so excited to see mature and be a focal point in my yard. I pruned it every year and tried to care for it the best I could. Over the years I started to see it leaning slightly. Each year the lean got more apparent. Finally I got down and started investigating what was happening with the roots to see if that was the cause. Sure enough, the roots were rotted and the entire tree was going to fall down eventually.

25

Pruning is important, but if the roots aren't strong in your family tree, it may just be a matter of time until it falls down.

In gathering information for my book, I decided to create a survey[1] that delved into the psyche of adults with regard to money behaviors. The results were very similar to the stories I'd heard from people over the years. The respondents ranged from ages 21 to 77. When asked what people's current financial concerns were, the overwhelming majority, *over 82 percent*, cited retirement planning as their biggest concern, with saving for emergencies closely behind. Additional concerns were paying bills, paying for education, healthcare and caring for an elderly family member. Budgeting is a factor that comes up with most families.

These are very real and impactful financial concerns. How we respond to and work through our matters has a ripple effect on those around us, especially our children. Most of the respondents learned about money from their parents. Friends, school, spouse and media almost tied as the answer to this question. One out of every four people surveyed felt *completely unprepared* for the financial responsibilities of adulthood, and about one-half felt only somewhat prepared. When questioned about retirement, 77 percent of the respondents indicated they were only somewhat prepared.

We need to better prepare the next generation for the financial world. Let's at least help the younger generation understand the basics and establish a strong foundation to build on throughout adulthood. We may be going through our day-to-day lives completely unaware of how much we're really watched by our children. I've tried to really keep this in mind when it comes to my daughter. Ever wondered where your child picked up a saying or a similar way of doing things? It is amazing how quickly they catch on.

---

[1] Anonymous survey completed through Survey Monkey, an online survey software and questionnaire tool. Respondents were able to complete and forward the survey for other individuals to complete. 163 individuals responded. Ages ranged from 21 to 77. Gender was 121 Female and 42 Male. Marital status was 107 currently married, 13 divorced, 43 never been married. 89 respondents have between 1 and 4 children. Child ages ranged between 1 and 48. Geographically located across the United States, Canada and Lebanon.

I'm not meaning to ask you to walk on water and part the seas to be parents. What I am asking is for YOU to be aware and demonstrate good decisions so that you can pass on those positive qualities. And if you do slip up, be quick to address it and show your child how resilient adults can be.

When asked how money was used in their family growing up, responses ranged from reward, guilt, autonomy, survival, joy, power, punishment and physical and emotional needs. Reward was the No.1 way money was used in these families. **How was it used in your family?** Ironically, when asked how money is *currently* used by the respondents, guess what came up on top? You guessed it: reward. There's no coincidence here. The ways money was used in our past is most often how it ranks at present. In my survey, "appearance" and "family and experiences" were the top ways money is currently used. Okay, so reward, experiences and appearance made it to the top of the list…interesting….

Next, I asked the question, "Growing up, you felt your parents spent a lot of money on_____." House and education came out on top. After digging a bit deeper, we sparked wonderful discussions of how the respondents thought their parents managed money well or how they spent it poorly. One respondent mentioned a pattern that was passed down from one generation to the next. Others cited the awareness that their parents were always living beyond their means or even wasting money, and many said their parents lived paycheck-to-paycheck. Some people thought their college education cost their parents their retirement or they wished their mother had worked to help pay the bills instead of staying home. Poor spending choices greatly affected one of the respondents. Their parents kept upgrading and trading up and it cost them personally in the end.

On the other end of the spectrum, many were aware of their parents managing their money well, living within their means, being frugal, taking their lunch to work every day, being well-insured, paying for things in cash, paying off debt and saving for retirement and education. Lessons learned from their parents ranged considerably. Positive lessons learned

were living within your means, saving for emergencies and retirement, giving to charity, the old axiom that money can't buy happiness and having a good, strong work ethic. I particularly enjoyed the response below from one respondent. He or she certainly had wonderful teachers.

> I was raised to 'never be in debt' and that's how we treated money. Earn it, save it, spend as necessary. The idea was to 'only spend what you have, and preferably spend less' so that you live within your means and have investments and retirement plans. The main point was 'if you never incur debt, you'll never have to dig out.' This has served me well! I had an allowance, and was given a credit card early at age 15 to learn how to use it wisely before being off on my own, and I do the same today. I was taught to understand finances and investments and to ask questions and make sure I understood the concepts, so that I would never feel powerless. My dad also required me to have a job during summers from age 16 onward, though I didn't need one, so I would learn what it was like to get a paycheck and see how taxes were taken out.

Another respondent recalled a very different lesson from their parents: "You can't take money to your grave, so spend it". That person cited their parents being poor now and unable to care for themselves. Some children were actually encouraged to take out debt in school to pay for what they wanted, over and above education. That person had over $10,000 in credit card debt when graduating from college. Other families just didn't talk about money at all:

> I think the only negative from growing up was that we just didn't talk about money. It was sort of a taboo subject. I knew

that they were very conscious of living within their means, but I did not get a lot of life lessons from them about the specifics of managing money, credit, taxes, mortgages, etc. It was all very hush-hush. I wish I would have learned more about the details.

A child's perceptions truly shape their personality and who they become. Respondents vividly remembered periods of unemployment for their parents where money was so scarce that the electricity was turned off, where they received calls from bill collectors and couldn't afford milk for the kids. Imagine a parent saying to their child, "DON'T PICK UP THE PHONE. We can't pay them."

Many recalled overhearing their parents' conversations. They heard about not having enough money to pay for what they needed that month, that "there just isn't enough to go around," or their parents saying they were poor or complaining that the child support just wasn't enough or that they couldn't pay the house payment that month. These children were there when the bank had to foreclose on their house or when they didn't have money for Christmas.

Some saw their mother spending money constantly redecorating their home and then later not being able to pay for groceries. A few people shared how money was used to address emotional problems in their families. If their parents fought, Mom went shopping. If you just needed to be cheered up, a shopping trip or just plain cash was the solution. We can't shelter our kids from all the stresses in life, but there are ways to better handle it for the benefit of your family and your children.

Positive memories were certainly there as well. Many recalled their parents talking to them about savings or taking them to the bank to open their first account and depositing money. Others remember grandparents discussing investments and giving to their church. Others detail doing chores for money, having small neighborhood jobs, and putting their coins into a money jar for savings.

One person surveyed recalled Dad reading *The Millionaire Next Door* by Thomas J. Stanley, Ph.D and William D. Danko, Ph.D (Thomas Stanley 3,4). In *The Millionaire Next Door*, the authors outline seven common denominators for the wealthy. Those factors ranged from living below their means, parents not providing economic outpatient care, adult children being economically self-sufficient and believing that financial independence is better than social status. The authors detail how "wealth is more often a result of a lifestyle of hard work, perseverance, planning, and, most of all, self-discipline."

I remember sitting at the kitchen table with my father. He was paying bills. The check register was out and his bills were all stacked in a pile. I asked what he was doing and wanted to be involved. Instead of putting me off for a while or telling me there was nothing to do, he gave me the stack of bills. He showed me how to look at the bill amount and where to write the amount on the check. I learned how to fill out the entire check, how to write out the words and double check that the numbers and written part matched. All he had to do was sign them. He ended by thanking me for all the help I'd been. I gained the knowledge of how to write out checks and started to understand where the money was being spent on things like electricity, car insurance and utilities. Take those opportunities with your children.

My next question in my survey was, "**How did your family environment affect your perceptions about money?**" The respondents had clear memories of the role money played in their childhood and how that affects them today. All but a few respondents said their childhood *directly* impacts how they view money today. Here is some of their advice:

- Always have a back-up plan
- Don't waste money
- Live within your means
- Don't express love with money

- ✺ I didn't have a grasp on money until it was coming out of my pocket
- ✺ Don't go into debt
- ✺ As an adult, I'm realizing how much money it costs to "have things"
- ✺ Live like the next Depression could happen any time
- ✺ Don't spoil your kids
- ✺ Retire debt-free
- ✺ Being "rich" has nothing to do with money
- ✺ You have to work hard to make money
- ✺ Be thankful for what you earn
- ✺ Start contributing to your retirement plan with your first paycheck
- ✺ Have parents give kids a budget if there is one, instead of promising something and then later not fulfilling it

This advice came from seeing both the good and bad circumstances in their families growing up. They heard, saw, lived and believed certain "truths" about what money meant to them and their families.

Some people feel that they are experiencing a financial trauma and there is no escape. "Catastrophe mode" is when you think that what you're facing is incomprehensible and inescapable. By seeking help, you will come to realize that many other individuals have been in your shoes before. You can begin to normalize your situation, which can give you some grounding. In a "normalized mode", you begin to realize that imminent death or catastrophe is not around the corner, and you can begin to see a clearer path and road map for finding your way toward being healthy and financially grounded.

From the financial perspective, an example of being in the catastrophe mode may be that debt has spiraled out of control, income isn't stable, investment portfolios are down and you feel that you are completely unable to control any part of your financial life. After this last recession, there are thousands of people who feel that they have experienced a financial

catastrophe. Hiding from the issues or internalizing the fear can hurt you emotionally, financially and physically. Fear can manifest itself in stomach issues, a flagging immune system, headaches, tension, sleep problems and more. Feel any of those symptoms?

You need a method to be able to address the emotional, financial and physical reactions. Get your team in place! You can meet with a therapist or support group to work through the psychological issues. Meet with your financial professional to help get you started on a solid plan that aligns your financial strategy with your goals. Most people feel that they need to have a lot of money to even talk with a financial professional, which is not the case at all. Some advisors do charge a minimum fee or require a minimum investment, but many can be paid hourly for advice. Last but certainly not least, contact your doctor to make sure the physical symptoms are addressed. Financial stresses can lead to high blood pressure, heart attacks and stomach ulcers, so make sure your healthcare professional is aware of any of the physical symptoms you've been having.

Often people seek help only after they've started experiencing the symptoms of financial struggles. They feel that there is only one area that is causing them concern and only want help addressing that one issue. It's important to look at the entire financial body. A similar example would be going to the doctor for a bruise that won't go away on your arm, but not allowing them to check your pulse and blood pressure at the visit. By doing a more thorough exam, it may be a systemic issue causing the bruising, the symptom. Until the systemic issue is addressed, the symptoms won't go away. If the systemic issue isn't addressed, your entire health may be at risk. If you don't address systemic financial issues, your entire financial health is at stake.

So many individuals believe they are "hard-wired" a certain way and they just can't change no matter how hard they try. That's a belief. The reality is actually the opposite, and there is research to prove it. Neuroplasticity is the brain's ability to reorganize itself by forming new neural connections. Nerve cells in the brain are able to adjust their activities in response to new situations or changes in the environment, thus allowing learning, adaptation and memory through new experiences. In *Train Your Mind, Change Your Brain* (Begley), Sharon Begley delves into how being mindful and focusing our attentions, we can change our brain structure to effect true change in emotional, cognitive and behavioral problems. "The brain can indeed be rewired…The adult brain, in short, retains much of the plasticity of the developing brain, including the power to repair damaged regions, to grow new neurons, to rezone regions that performed one task and have them assume a new task, to change the circuitry that weaves neurons into the networks that allow us to remember, feel, suffer, think, imagine and dream. Yes, the brain of a child is remarkably malleable. But…the brain can change its physical structure and its wiring long into adulthood." (Begley 8)

Change is difficult for some, but the act of intentionally changing experiences, behaviors and actions can help not only reshape our thoughts, but can actually reshape our brain. The results can be life changing. I want this book to help you with something priceless: being a healthy individual who can change your life for the better, model positive influences and behaviors for your children and steward them through the process of growth. My goal is to help this generation and future generations of people roll up their sleeves and do the work to have meaningful, healthy and happy lives.

Dr. Carl Rogers is considered to be one of the most influential psychologists of the 20th century. Dr. Rogers believed in the power of human potential and famously said, "The curious paradox is that when I accept myself just as I am, then I can change."

Determine what your beliefs are and look at them objectively. Where are you headed? Just like going on a trip, you need to decide what to pack. If you don't want to lug your baggage around anymore, then leave

it behind. It's what I like to call "checking your baggage at the door." If you don't, over time you will start to feel the weight of the world on your shoulders, the excess baggage. Your journey will become more and more difficult, and you'll be limiting your true potential. Imagine taking a day trip to the mountains where you have to carry all of your baggage on your back. If you're lugging around a heavy load, you can only go so far before you need to stop and rest. Maybe it becomes so challenging that you put your bags down and sit out the rest of the day. How much of the world have you seen on your trip?

Now imagine you're carrying a fairly light load. You start up the mountain, stopping only on occasion to catch your breath. At the end of the day, you've made it to the top of the mountain and see the most spectacular view you've ever seen in your life. Your legs feel a bit tired from the hike, but your blood is flowing, your heart is pumping and the breeze is cooling you and bringing fresh new air into your lungs. You feel *alive*. You sit and gaze into the beauty that is all around you. Had your load been too heavy, none of this would have been possible. Which journey are you on?

You have a wonderful opportunity TODAY to find peace within yourself, improve your family's financial situation and, most of all, plant good seeds for your children to grow into financially healthy adults. Realize that you don't need to stay stuck. Dr. Klontz discussed various money disorders he has researched. "Workaholism denies friends and family members of the kind of interaction they want/desire with a loved one. What friends/family need from the workaholic is their presence. What they get is economic (presents). The latter can never satisfy the former. Financial enabling is primarily found when parents financially support their adult children, creating a 'false economy,' in the sense that their children are able to live a lifestyle that is artificially created by parental support. It keeps the children dependent, 'little' and immature, irresponsible, and ultimately, in most cases, resulting in disaster when the parent's money runs out or the children are 'cut off'."

Anything hit home? Until you face the issues and deal with them, you have what's called "unfinished business." If we don't resolve our issues, they stay with us, seeping into our present lives and relationships, and can interfere with our growth and happiness–they are just weeds. You not only affect yourself, you pass along those seeds to your children and those unhealthy habits continue living on from one generation to the next. In being true with yourself, face the fear, whatever is driving the behavior and develop an action plan for change.

I read an excerpt from a book about financial planning titled *Women's Worth: Finding Your Financial Confidence* (Blayney), by Eleanor Blayney, which offers a great analogy concerning money: "Money is nothing and everything; actually it's just grease. It does not do anything on its own, but properly used with foresight and reason, it makes things happen, makes things go. By itself, it's a toxic substance and can be very messy. Applied sensibly on a routine basis, it can make life run more smoothly."

Money can be used in many ways—for greed, for status, for respect, for charity, for education and for daily living. Money is something that we think about every day. It comes up in our paycheck, putting gas in our car, buying groceries, adjusting the thermostat in your home to save a little and paying for the water to run through our plumbing. It's how we use it in our life that shapes how we set a new belief system for generations to come. That, in and of itself, is a true parental responsibility. Take guidance from Deuteronomy 4:9: "Only be careful, and watch yourselves closely so that you do not forget the things your eyes have seen or let them fade from your heart as long as you live. Teach them to your children and to their children after them."

Digging In The Dirt

It's amazing how wonderful our minds can be. We really do have the power to start or stop a habit just by thinking differently. It's that complex and that simple all at the same time. We can reshape our minds and forge new paths for our futures. First, we need to explore your true, authentic self values, which are where your financial decisions are rooted. What values are most and least important to you?

Acceptance, acknowledgement, adventure, affection, ambition, affluence, awareness, balance, beauty, bravery, bliss, candor, capability, certainty, care, clarity, cleanliness, comfort, completion, confidence, contribution, creativity, decisiveness, dependability, desire, duty, education, efficiency, endurance, enjoyment, entertainment, extravagance, fairness,

fashion, financial independence, fitness, flexibility, freedom, fun, giving, grace, gregariousness, happiness, health, holiness, humor, hygiene, imagination, impact, insightfulness, intimacy, inventiveness, investing, joy, justice, kindness, knowledge, longevity, loyalty, love, making a difference, order, peace, perseverance, philanthropy, pleasure, popularity, power, pragmatism, preparedness, realism, reason, relaxation, reliability, resilience, respect, rest, sacrifice, security, sharing, significance, simplicity, spirit, stability, support, success, thankfulness, thoroughness, tranquility, trust, truth, understanding, usefulness, virtue, warmth, wealth, wisdom, youthfulness

Which values speak to you? You'll find that's typically where the money goes. If it's not, there can be that feeling that something is just off, missing. How well do you feel your values line up with your financial behavior? Are you financially healthy? A clear picture of your value system will allow for better decisions. Write out all of the values listed above on note cards and pick out which ones match you. Sort them from most important to you to least important. What are your top five? On the back of each card, write down what you are doing to shine light for that value in your life. For example, if your value is integrity and you work in an environment that doesn't support or encourage ethics, you can truly feel the dissonance. It's that "something just doesn't feel right" feeling that tells you that your behaviors are misaligned with your values.

Is family a value for you? What are you doing with respect to that value, and how does your financial behavior encourage it? One of my values is family. My financial behavior to support that value is having a properly implemented financial plan. I have life insurance so that if I pass away my family would not be financially devastated and my daughter could still continue her education.[2] Education is a value of mine, so I set aside money every month in a college plan for my daughter and make sacrifices in other areas to pay for her schooling.

I understand the importance of those values to me, and I have made sacrifices. It's amazing how people will say how much they value their families, yet have absolutely no life insurance coverage. Be sure to find out which type is best for your situation. There are so many types of coverage to meet different budgets and needs that there really isn't an excuse not to have it. Some excuses I've heard over the years involve the cost or that nobody should "benefit" from someone else's death. The reality is that if you don't make it home *today*, your family will be emotionally devastated. Now fast forward to *tomorrow* when the mortgage still needs to be paid and the tuition is still due.

Life continues for those left behind, and you are no longer there to contribute your paycheck. Maybe you even left some debt behind. Maybe there were medical bills to be paid or a funeral to pay for. Are you content with the fact that your family would also be financially devastated? If you don't work, do you need coverage? YES, some. If you stay home and care for the household, your spouse will have to pay someone else to help with the house, picking up the kids and so forth. People who have experienced the loss of a parent at an early age are far more likely to value having good life insurance. They relied on that to pay for their everyday living expenses. Here are two very different scenarios: One father had life insurance and the policy proceeds paid for the costs of living, education and the widowed spouse's retirement. Scenario 2: A father passed away without life insurance and the family had to make financial sacrifices including considering selling their home and the mother had to take on a second job to pay the bills. Would finding some money in the budget to get a "do-over" and change from the second scenario to the first be worth it?

---

2   Life insurance products contain fees, such as mortality and expense charges, and may contain restrictions, such as surrender periods.

In each case, the emotional trauma was clearly present. One family was spared the financial trauma while the other lived it. Life is about choices. If family, peace of mind and financial security are a value to you, then having adequate life insurance matches your values to your financial strategy.

The same case can be applied to disability insurance. If either parent were unable to work, you would want a policy with a benefit to provide some replacement income in the event of a disability. It's important to review your coverage to see how much of an income you'd receive if you lost your ability, either temporarily or permanently, to work and bring home an income. However, according to the Council for Disability Awareness, every second another disabling injury occurs, and 90 percent are NOT work-related (Awareness). If you think you are covered by your policy at work, you might want to double-check to see whether that policy covers non-work related injuries. Many people have disability coverage through their employer.

Some plans offer the option to buy supplemental coverage beyond the basic plan benefit. Review your company's Summary Plan Description document for information about the plan options. Inquire into the cost of supplemental coverage and what you'd be eligible for. Both life and disability insurance that are employer-paid would be taxable income to you or your beneficiaries if you became disabled or passed away. See if your employer will allow the premium payments to be paid by you from your paycheck. This would allow the benefits then to be tax-free to you or your beneficiaries. You would rather pay small income tax on the premiums than on the benefits received. If you are self-employed or run a business, you need to get the coverage for yourself as well as covering the company's overhead. If you're the only one running the show, you don't want to have your business go down the drain along with the income you would no longer be making. You may have to sell your business and face the risk of getting a lower value due to timing. Determine if this is a value for you and your family.

Both cultural and community values may influence what you feel your values should be. You may live in a community that values material possessions. There may be external pressure for you to live a certain life-style in order to be accepted, and for many people, acceptance from a social circle or community is important. Maybe you want to live in an exclusive neighborhood or drive a luxury car. Make sure the payments and long-term commitment can be met without sacrificing your other values. I've seen time and time again when people will tell me their values are education for their children and financial well-being. The interesting part to me is that they are willing to pay top dollar for a luxury car, country club membership or large home, but they "don't have enough money" to save for education, savings or retirement. The reality is that they value status and acceptance over education and financial well-being because that is where their money is going.

Marketing and Values

Marketing has a huge impact on our spending behaviors. Companies pay hundreds of thousands of dollars to convince people that all of their problems will be solved if they buy X, Y or Z. Just think about how many diet plan commercials you've seen over the years. I can think of hundreds. They're catering to people who want an "easy" way to drop those unwanted pounds, become more successful and happier than ever imagined. The reality is that losing weight involves some basic steps that do involve work: a healthy diet and exercise. Marketing campaigns will cater to your inner most thoughts. They empathize with how long you spend in your car and tell you that you deserve to spend your time in luxury. Make sure you can afford the car payment without sacrificing other values.

Another primary goal of marketing is to create a "need" where one does not exist. Companies do this by trying to stimulate a sense of fear in a

consumer that if they do not have the product, something bad will happen to them. A good example of this is the growth of anti-bacterial soap and other products over the last decade. For several thousand years, humans have survived with regular soap and water. There are no more bacteria now than in the past. In fact, some researchers have concluded that using anti-bacterial soap actually harms your body by making bacteria resistant to such products.

Talk with your kids about what marketing they see and what they think. How did it affect their buying behavior, and how did it affect their personal values? Just by watching a football game your child will be subjected to beer commercials with scantily clad women. Talk with your children about the commercial even though you may feel a bit uncomfortable doing it. Your son or daughter observes these images, so you need to be able to help them process what they mean. Your daughter will be receiving messages early on from all media outlets showing tall, thin women looking rather sexy. You want to help her see that this is marketing to a certain demographic and that normal women do not look like that nor should they dress in that manner (and that inner-beauty is more important than outer-beauty).

If you don't address these issues, your children may soon be dealing with eating disorders, promiscuity and worse. Your son may feel that in order to feel successful, he must be a beer-drinking athlete who wins every game or feels he needs to be the bully. His view of how his future love interests look and act are influenced by these images as well.

The fallacy is that these images are creating an unrealistic model of how people should look, be and act. Open the dialogue with your children about what impressions you have about what you are seeing. Even the most level-headed, pragmatic kids will be affected, so don't assume they won't be. If you do not counter the messages your children are getting from commercials, television shows and the media, they will adopt those values.

However, children are smart and can usually tell the difference between fiction and reality. The important part is to make sure that your children know what version of reality should be the standard.

Talk to most anyone I know and they'll tell you I've got some pretty thick skin. This is surely the case now, and it has been for most of my life. I can admit that even I have questioned myself over the years as I've compared myself to others and to images from the media. I'm reminded of how I'm not the "normal" height every time I buy a pair of pants. I am 5'4" tall, and the average pant is made for taller women. I have to have every pant tailored about two to three inches shorter, and petit sizes don't fit well either.

Look at the magazines targeting women. In 2009, a story headlined about a model who was fired for being too fat. She was 5'10" and weighed 120 pounds. According to Weight Watchers, someone 5'10" should ideally weigh from 139 to 174. Don't you think it's important to talk with your daughter about healthy body image? If you don't, she's going to get her information from elsewhere—her friends and media. Yikes!

My daughter was given a Barbie Doll by a friend when she was 2 years old. At first, I was happy for her since I remember playing with Barbie Dolls when I was a child. Barbie and Ken had a great time in the Dream House and Fun Times RV, all memories from the 1970s. In recollection, I was much older than 2 when playing with them. My 2 year old enjoyed taking Barbie's clothes off and leaving her naked around the house. In doing my usual sweep of her toys to clean up, I'd notice the buxom plastic blonde staring up at me from the couch or the floor and I actually felt slightly uncomfortable. Did I want my daughter getting the message that women really look like that? According to a March 2009 report from BBC News titled, *What would a real Barbie look like?*, academics from the University of South Australia suggest the likelihood of a woman having Barbie's body shape is one in 100,000, and researchers at Finland's University Central

Hospital in Helsinki say, "If Barbie were life size she would lack the 17 to 22 percent body fat required for a woman to menstruate." (Winterman) You want to send the correct messages early on so that when these external sources come into play your children will know how to respond and how to stay true to their values. Start the dialogue.

Do you value being financially independent when you are no longer working? What does your vision of retirement look like? I know, you're reading a book about planting savings seeds and growing financially savvy children and we're talking about *your* retirement. Your roots affect the structure of the family money tree. There will come a time when you are either forced by an employer to retire, you are no longer able to keep working due to age or illness or you die while on the job. You need to put money aside for yourself for later down the road. I know that raising kids is expensive, especially if you have multiple children or are a single parent. You need to think of yourself and plan for a time when the only income may be from what you've saved.

I remember when my daughter was potty-trained and the weekly trip for diapers was no longer on our to-do list, nor was a $100 per month expense. Just after she was born, I remember gasping at how many diapers infants go through in a day. Little did I know that expense would be replaced with schooling. The key is that you need to find some money that can be put into retirement savings, and then help pay for college with what's left. I've seen countless parents who didn't, and they lost the benefit of time, income earning years and interest and found themselves scrambling to pay for their retirement. Show your children the importance of saving for retirement. You will want to be able to pay for your care when you are no longer working.

Some people may have a hefty forthcoming family inheritance. You know who you are. Your family has money, and your retirement plan is sticking around long enough and playing nice at family get-togethers to remain a part of your family's estate plan. You think you're going to inherit money and that's what's going to float you through the golden years. Guess what? That story may play out differently. It's not YOUR money after all, and plans can change. I've seen massive amounts of wealth that people were *counting* on go to charities, new spouses (that may not be much older than you) and to pay for the long-term care needs for the actual owner of those assets—not you. Your retirement plan should not be based on someone else's reversible decisions.

There is another group of people worth mentioning whose mantra is, "Everything always works out in the end so I don't need to plan. Live for today!" *Carpe diem* sounds so romantic and whimsical, doesn't it? I am sometimes jealous of that group. Ignorance is bliss, right? Not really. There are too many folks who DIDN'T plan ahead and they ran out of money living their final days impoverished, passing along a nice chunk of debt to the ones left behind.

Would you make a change here and there so that you could spend your later years with dignity? Hindsight really is 20/20, and if you could fast forward as if in a movie and see how everything played out, I bet your older self would counsel you on why the "wants" of your younger years don't outweigh the "needs" of your later years. It's your choice.

Plant the saving seed in your children as early as possible and show them what it's like to save by doing it for yourself. A child can open a ROTH IRA and contribute as long as they have earned income. Many young adults graduate from college and retirement savings is the farthest thought in their mind. The reality is that with their very first job, a minimum of 10 percent of their gross pay should be set aside for retirement. Getting a late start means either needing to save even more down the road or possibly downgrading their goals and lifestyles.

An interesting observation is seeing someone who's just started out in the working world who may tend to feel like retirement is so far down the road that it isn't even a blip on the radar. Ask someone who's worked 10 years or longer and they'd probably say they'd like to be able to quit working sooner rather than later. It sure would be nice to have the option, wouldn't it? Your child seeing you set money aside every month for your goals certainly influences their sense of normalcy when it comes to their future planning.

Is education a value for you? Tie your financial strategy to your education goals with proper college and education planning for your children and possibly your grandchildren. Kids today need a minimum of a college degree, if not further graduate-level courses, to be competitive in the work force. If this is a value, align your budget to include education planning. Luck wasn't involved when you magically went to college "all bills paid." Many parents or grandparents footed the bill. Now, pay it forward.

Counterpoint: So, you worked through college and paid your own way through. You probably learned life lessons beyond comparison. That's great. And teaching the same lesson may be very important to you. Then great. I'd still advise you to put away a little if you can for a backup. It may soften the landing a bit for them later. Historically, the college tuition inflation rate is about double what the consumer price index is in our country. It costs more and more every year to educate our children, so every bit helps.

Let me give some guidance to address the beliefs we discussed earlier. Try these out.

- If you don't have the money to buy something that's a want and not a need, don't buy it. Be clear about *need* versus *want*.

- Your lifestyle should reflect where you are financially, not the lifestyle you grew up in or the lifestyle of those around you.

- We all work hard; it's part of life. If you don't have the money for something, don't take on debt for it.

- Redefine your view of success. Success can't be bought, and having more things doesn't equate to more success.

- If you feel guilty working, spend more time with your family instead of using money to show affection. Find good family activities you can do around town.

- Even if only one person works outside the home, both partners should make the financial decisions together. Both parents should be involved and on the same page.

- Communicate and talk about money in your family.

- Put together an accountability group if needed. Start a group of friends who are all committed to improving their financial life. Surround yourself with a community that supports your efforts and wants you to succeed.

Remember our earlier discussion about brain plasticity? Our actions and experiences shape our brain and either grow or prune neural connections. The old adage of "you are what you eat" can actually be understood as "you are what you think." Start with yourself and work with your children to start good habits and better experiences to improve your thoughts and your mind. Bad habits and negative thoughts are mapped as well, so be mindful of what you are allowing in your brain and those of your household. Bad habits turn into weeds and can impair those other positive seedlings from growing.

We need to be very honest with ourselves about how we see money and how we use it. For some, it may involve facing some extremely tough realities such as stirring painful childhood memories or other dark times in your

life. It is actually very liberating and there is a feeling of a weight being lifted once you really confess to yourself (and others) what the money issue is and where it came from. Confront the past in order to unfetter yourself to move forward.

I understand that this all seems like it would be heard in a psychologist's office and not in a book about families and money. Our actions with our children, teaching the good lessons and backing them up speak volumes to your children. *Parenting With Confidence*, a parenting workshop created by Focus on the Family, cites five basic needs of children: acceptance, affection, attention, affirmation and accountability. I really thought about those needs with regard to my life and my daughter. Gosh, if I can get those A's down pat, I will be the best parent and my daughter would be well on her way to blossoming into a well-balanced adult.

How fulfilling and wonderful would it be for a child:

- To feel accepted unconditionally and affirmed by their parents?
- To get positive attention and quality time together?
- To be shown true affection through interaction?
- To be held and to hold their parents accountable?

If we're honest with ourselves, wouldn't getting acceptance, affection, attention, affirmation and accountability from our parents have been fulfilling? Guess what? Those are free. The only cost on your part is effort through spending time with your child, being engaged and supportive. Write those five A's down and post them on the refrigerator or your bathroom mirror as a reminder. Our busy lives can distract us from the important lessons right in front of us. Ask any adult if their favorite memories were from a certain gift or from an experience where they felt loved and fulfilled by a parent. The experience wins out every time.

Figure out what your "financial stuff" is, face it and use that lesson to help teach your child something invaluable. Maybe freeing yourself will allow you more room for acceptance, affection, attention, affirmation and accountability with your child. I hear a John Lennon song coming on, "Imagine all the people…" That would be awesome.

When I told people I was writing this book, it's like they were compelled to start sharing their past financial experiences. It's cathartic to talk about and share our stories and I encourage that dialogue for you. These stories are very real. People would tell me vividly the memories they had decades ago. Clearly their experiences left a lasting impression, ones they easily remembered both the details and the feelings associated with them.

There were many who felt that they didn't have much growing up and, now that they have an income, they feel that they deserve to have the "wants" in their life, whether it is expensive shoes, $250 a month in coffee, luxury cars or large homes. Some just get the big-ticket items while others spend their money on lots of small things and some like the shopping for the thrill.

The other group got most of what they wanted when they were growing up. Parents paid the tab and all was gravy. Now, these people have grown up and don't understand why they have to "downgrade" from their previous standard of living now that they are footing the bill. If you're used to square footage, top-shelf electronics, nice cars, designer clothes and a hefty bank account, there's a rude awakening about to happen if that's the expectation and you don't have the income or assets to afford it. It hits the ego pretty hard, and depending on the person, they either start to live within their means or they try to keep up with the Joneses and dig deeper into debt just to maintain the lifestyle. That lifestyle doesn't last forever, and that's a hard road to go down.

Keeping up with the Joneses is hard on families. Parents stress about paying the bills, all the while trying to keep their public image of happiness and affluence polished. The kids get a false sense of what's real and learn to expect those luxuries. Adding to the anxiety is the feeling that you will fail the kids if you don't keep it up or that you will lose your friends. The game has to end at some point and you'll wish you could teleport yourself back to make some different choices. Often, living this "double life" can cause marital tensions and many times those stresses can lead to divorce. Not the road you want to go down...

In my survey I asked this important question: "What do you WISH you would have been taught about money?" After all, hindsight is 20/20, isn't it? Maybe we can learn something here through their stories and experiences. Of this group, about 53 percent felt money was tight growing up. They wish they'd learned to—

- Balance a checkbook
- Run a monthly budget and live on that budget
- Use credit wisely, as well as the importance of paying off the bill every month
- Invest properly
- Save, starting early in life
- Give to charity or religious organizations
- Resist the temptation to buy something just because it's on sale
- Talk about money
- Plan a balanced life
- Take emotion out of financial decisions
- Value the work involved in earning money
- Develop a strong work ethic
- Save early for retirement
- Understand how money truly works, how it grows and how damaging it can be to your life if you misuse it

What wonderful gems of wisdom.

What lessons did *I* learn as a child about money? How does that impact how I see money now? I had always been the child who ran a lemonade stand or oversold at garage sales (Mom, sorry again for selling your designer chair for $5). I had been working as a babysitter and earning money since I can remember. Early on, making money was just for the fun of it. I came to realize that I may just need to have some extra cash to pay for some of the "wants."

I really didn't mind working; it actually felt good to learn a new skill and also comforting to add to a savings cushion. A positive side effect was my having experience in the workplace, which helped later on in my adult career. Two lessons I learned: Always have some money in the bank and live at a level you can afford even if you had to downsize. Really nobody in October, 2007 thought that the stock market would fall over 50 percent, that unemployment would be over 10 percent and so many financial scandals would be uncovered. Not having some money in the bank AND losing a job AND your house? Thousands of people found themselves in that exact situation.

Go talk with someone who lived during the Depression or who was raised by someone from the Depression. That generation had to truly learn the value of the dollar. People worked in whatever capacity they could just to put food on their family's tables. Today, we tend to wait until the better job comes along instead of getting any job we can to provide for ourselves or draw out unemployment benefits as a way of gaining some free time off of work. There has been a financial evolution over the last 50 years, and I don't know if it's really for the better. In the olden days, it was unheard of to buy a house without putting at least 20 percent down. That house was on average about 1,200 square feet in size, and the kids shared rooms and bathrooms. Media rooms were not even conceived—kids played outside.

Today, the average home size is 2,100 square feet, with many homes well over that. We've super-sized ourselves, and that goes along with our debt. People drove cars until the car went kaput and only then replaced them, often paying cash. This past recession has made more people aware of certain extravagances, and many are cutting back. The larger homes are being passed over for something smaller, more energy efficient and easier to maintain. Let's hope that trend continues and our memories stay fresh.

What lessons can you teach your children about this time? I encourage older family members and community members to share their stories with the younger generation. Hearing from someone who has been there is more impactful than reading some history book.

When I was in elementary school, we had to do a project on family history. My grandparents each wrote letters about what it was like growing up. My grandparents grew up during the Depression. They wrote about food rationing and grocery vouchers. There were lines to get food and supplies. Hearing their stories in detail made it real.

What lesson are you teaching your children by NOT discussing money or planting healthy financial seeds? It's much the same as not talking with your children about other topics—they learn it from outside sources. Maybe you are talking with your children, but aren't being clear with your message. Which is better, coming from you or your child's best friend whose dad drives a Porsche and has some offshore business and apparently a tree in the backyard that grows money? Be honest with your children about your financial experience when you feel they are old enough to understand. Start money discussions early, such as, "Do you know where Mommy and Daddy go when you're at school?" Explain about all the fun and important things you do at your job or at home. You can weave in the concept of pay by letting them know that as compensation for all the hard work you did at work, you were paid money. Then explain that money is used to buy things and to pay for services. For example, "When Mommy gets paid, I use that money to buy food to eat and for the clothes we wear. Daddy's pay is used to pay for our house and feed the dog." You can let your child know that you save a little away for future expenses every time you get paid. We're reinforcing what we ask them to do with their allowance by what we do with our income.

I know by now that many of you reading this are saying, "Great, but easier said than done." Trust me, I know firsthand about coming home from work to find the dog sick ($300 vet bill) and the hot water heater going out ($650 bill) all in a day, not to mention you have your child in tow. I love talking with my clients about the importance of emergency reserves. They either think, *It will never happen to me*, and they carry on unconcerned and being content with less savings, or they come from life-can-throw-stuff-at-you-in-an-instant-and-you-need-some-cash-to-pay-for-it camp. The difference is you've either had something happen or you haven't…yet.

Usually you change camps with the purchase of a new house. That's why the first time something goes wrong at your home, established home-owners get this grin on their faces and issue the ever-famous expression, "Ah, the joys of homeownership." You get really tired of hearing that after a few times, but it's true. Homeownership is not always a joyful experience. One piece of advice, the day you get the keys to your house, go to the home improvement store and buy a water key. If a pipe bursts, the dishwasher or the hot water heater goes out, that key can turn the water off to your house. Find out where the water valve is in your yard and remember where you keep the key. Water damage can be costly and insurance may not cover what you think it will.

The assumptions we make about how life is going to play out can really be way off the mark. There are just so many stories of events that just took people to their knees. Wham! We didn't expect 12.5 inches of snow in Dallas, Texas in one day, but it happened in 2010. The most snow in

Dallas' history. It was actually rather beautiful at first. We had a fire in the fireplace, were watching DVDs and drinking hot apple cider. Then the power went out, tree limbs crashed into our roof from the weight of the snow and we were stuck in the house, unable to drive the roads. Costs: tree trimming and removal, replenishing spoiled groceries from the refrigerator and freezer and minor house repairs. Think of the areas in the country that have been hit by snowstorms, flooding, oil spills and tornados. Stuff happens, so you need savings. Depending on the severity of your "opportunities for patience," as I like to call them, you either are okay with six months of expenses set aside in savings or you'd rather have more. At the very least, have enough to cover insurance, annual deductibles on health plans, one percent of the value in your home for home maintenance and three months of living expenses.

Planting Pairs

My any marriages and relationships struggle with money issues. You're joining two people in a relationship, and money beliefs and spending and savings habits may not be in line. So, how do you take *mine* and *yours* and make it *ours*? Lisa Perry, founder of *The Well Blended Family*, an organization to help divorced and blended families flourish, can attest that finances can definitely affect blended families. According to Lisa Perry, "Probably the most significant mistake I see blended families make regarding finances is the "yours & mine" mentality. My husband and I made that mistake in the beginning. I always say the difference between the mindset of getting into a first marriage and second marriage goes something like this: Before our first marriage we are usually saying to ourselves "I am so excited! I can't wait to get married! This is going to be forever. . . . !" If we are bold enough to try it again after the dissolution of our first marriage, the thoughts go more like this "I hope this one goes

better than the last!" In second marriages - often - our guard is up. We are feeling protective of what we have — kids, property and finances. We don't want anything taken away from us again. So, I see these weird financial arrangements that have a positive intention of protecting one's assets (and guarding from future losses), however, the results are usually difficulties in budgeting, and spending and saving conflicts, especially when it comes to each other's children. Every couple is unique in their scenario and what they come into the new marriage with and without. There still needs to be a "grand plan" that is not splintered. The couple needs to spend time developing a vision of their future together that combines both of their desires both for themselves and their kids." (Perry)

Lisa Perry lists five of the most common mistakes in blending families:

1. Parent over/under functioning

2. Discount the "Step" role

3. Over-indulging children

4. Misplaced frustration/anger/resentment

5. Discount your own power

The first mistake describes one parent who does most of the "heavy lifting." They take the primary responsibility for a whole host of issues. In divorced families, you commonly see one of the biological parents take on more of the financial responsibility, make excuses for the other parent not keeping promises and making sure calendars and schedules are tended to. In blended families, you commonly see the biological parent taking on more responsibilities as a result of guilt or fear of burdening the non-biological parent.

The second mistake involves a step-parent taking a backseat to parenting and disciplining their non-biological children as not feeling they

have the right to parent the child. Financially, there will tend to be a "mine" and "yours" mentality when considering the money. The biological parent might take more of a "my way" attitude when it comes to spending/saving money regarding their children without the concurrence of the step-parent and/or the step-parent may be reluctant to participate financially in the child's welfare.

After a divorce, parents may feel guilt, resulting in the third mistake of over-indulging their children as a way of compensating for the inferred pain they caused their children. Over-indulgence can also show itself in creating a "comfortable" new environment or trying to emulate an old environment after a divorce. Common phrases from such a parent may be, "But they've been through so much already..." or "So much has changed in our lives that I want us to live in the same neighborhood and have the same type of house that we had as a family so that not too much is different for them." Filling the void left from an ended relationship cannot be filled with temporal things. There was a trauma that occurred and it takes healing, not over-indulgence.

Misplacing emotions involves expressing those negative emotions with one family member when in actuality, it is another family member that one has issue with. You may see this with a step-parent taking frustration out on the child instead of their new spouse. It's important to be mindful of the whirlwind of feelings and emotions and where they should be directed.

The Five Essential Elements for Blending Families that Lisa describes are:

1. Relationship/marriage as the center of the family unit

2. Step-parent role is a parenting role

3. Solid "House Rules"

4. Always focused on a WIN-WIN-WIN

5. Seek support and guidance

All families start with a couple. "The relationship should be the nucleus of the family and their children, parents and friends become the satellite relationships. Having a respectful, loving and supportive relationship provides that sense of security for the children and helps them to develop healthy boundaries" counsels Lisa. A step-parent is still a parent. With that comes respect and adherence to the family rules. Well-blended families have established guidelines and strategies focused on creating structure and balance for the entire family. House rules involve respect, integrity, responsibility and security for all family members.

Lisa describes the WIN-WIN-WIN as finding the positive intention in you, the ex and the kids. "This requires a bit of empathy, but this Essential Element alone is the magic key to creating peace and cohesiveness in both your family and between households," says Lisa Perry. Her last Essential Element is just as crucial. "Successfully blended families know that they don't have all the answers and sometimes need a little help and support. They actively seek help when they need it which can be anything from babysitting options for "relationship" time, to hiring professionals to resolve problems and develop better communication skills. We were not born knowing everything. Sometimes we just have to ask for help!"

Be open with each other about your money situation. Discuss the good, the bad and the very ugly. This gives a clearer, honest picture as well as openness between each other. The other person should understand the position you're in as a couple and what that means to your family and lifestyle. You don't want to be in a heap of debt or living beyond your means and try to give the illusion you're peachy. I recommend each person pulling their credit report every year and each year sitting down with your partner or spouse and swap reports. Understand not only what your

credit history is but also understand what your significant other owes and to whom they owe it. Having your partner on the same page will make it easier to understand the financial decisions since you'll be making them together. You don't want to find out during a mortgage application process that the other person on the loan has mounting debt and multiple debtors that you didn't know about. You can pull a free annual credit report every year. According to the Federal Trade Commission (Commission), "AnnualCreditReport.com is the ONLY authorized source to get your free annual report under federal law."

In bringing two people together in a relationship, you're not only bringing two people into the equation, you're bringing in two, possibly very different, personality types. Find out what your personality type is as well as that of your new partner so you each can understand each other better and work to compliment each other's styles as opposed to picking out characteristics that you love and try to fix the ones you don't. Some popular tests are the DISC Personality System and the Myers-Briggs® Personality Test. You may be a Driver who is direct and decisive and your partner may be an Influencer who is more emotional. These are both good qualities—but if misunderstood may cause tension. The Driver's directness may be alluring early on in the relationship, but may be misunderstood as lack of emotion which can conflict with the Influencer's needs. A better understanding of each other will go quite far in planting pairs. Take it a bit further and add some extra fertilizer. Get to know each other's love languages. Dr. Gary Chapman, author of *The 5 Love Languages* (Chapman), discusses five things that make us feel loved: Words of Affirmation, Quality Time, Receiving Gifts, Acts of Service and Physical Touch. Find out how you each feel loved.

If you're coming into the relationship with children, maybe thus far you've each raised your children with a certain set of rules and those are not in sync with your new partner. These are discussions that really need to

happen in the dating phase. I say this for more than the money issue. You each need to be clear about your beliefs and family needs before entering a new relationship and affecting your children. The purpose of your conversation is not to attack or make your point for the millionth time. The point of communication is to have a better understanding of each other. Be clear about your money from the beginning.

As a woman, I can have a hard time with this. I am speaking in generalities, but you'll get the point. Often women like to talk things out. We can get with our girlfriends to talk, listen and give feedback. We gain energy from talking and feel closeness by being heard just by having the conversation. For men, this can be a stressful and an energy-draining experience. Men often like to get to the point in as straightforward a path as possible. There's a problem? Tell me what it is and let's fix it. Women like to talk about all the ways to see the problem, talk about their feelings, know that they are being understood and feel more emotionally connected after the talk. Talking for a long period of time may actually have the opposite effect on a man. After a long talk, he may want to be alone or do another activity to reenergize his mind. He may feel attacked, feeling responsibility for not being able to immediately "fix" the problem that was brought up in the conversation, which may increase his need for isolation.

Make sure you are communicating what you are truly meaning to communicate. Dr. Albert Mehrabian, in his book, *Silent Messages* (Mehrabian), concluded that *only 7 percent* of what is communicated is actually the words we say, what is verbalized. The overwhelming majority, 93 percent, is 38 percent tone (vocal liking) and 55 percent body language (facial liking). Have your conversation in person with an awareness of tone and body language, or else 93 percent of what you talk about may be misunderstood. Email and texting are great for non-subjective information but can get you in a pickle. By picking up the phone, whether in personal or business relationships, you at least increase your chances of being understood

by 38 percent through your tone. Ideally, you'd like to have a one-on-one discussion in person. You have eye contact, affirmation of understanding through nodding and can sense if you're not on the same page through stiffening of your posture or facial expressions.

A good solution is to have some ground rules for your conversations. James 1:19 (*NIV*) states, "My dear brothers, take note of this: Everyone should be quick to listen, slow to speak and slow to become angry."

Rule 1: Set a reasonable time limit for the talk. Stick to the time limit and mute all interruptions (phone, email, etc.). You may decide that a 30-minute talk is best. You will know that you each need to be present and an active listener for 30 minutes.

Rule 2: Have an agenda and take turns. Keep your conversations to a topic so that you know what will be addressed. If something else comes up, put it on the agenda for your next conversation. The first point on your agenda should be what each of you would like to get out of the talk and what your expectations are. Just as an example, a wife's expectations may just be that she wants to be heard and know that her husband understands where she's coming from. If that's not clear, her husband, loving her dearly and wanting to come to the rescue, may chime in with all the ways to fix the problem. There may have been nothing to fix; rather, she wanted to feel love by being heard. His well-meaning solutions may come across as unloving because she isn't getting her needs met. By stating expectations, the conversation can be effective and clear. She can express her feelings with him actively listening instead of partially listening while getting his solution list in his head. He can then end the conversation by thanking her for being open and recapping what he understood so that she knows he heard her and she feels loved. Turn it around the other way now. Maybe his expectations of the conversation are to get to the point and get some solutions. She will understand this from the beginning and not be upset when

he's asking for decisive answers without a lengthy discussion about it and he will get his answers and feel respected for getting his needs met.

Rule 3: Like your vitamins, keep it to one a day. You want to allow time for rest. Having more than one scheduled talk in a day can be draining and can muddy the waters if too many topics are buzzing around in your head. Maybe your talk hit a hot button for one of you. If you don't give it time for reflection and digestion, you may bring those feelings into the next talk even if they have no place there.

Rule 4: Keep it clean. There should be no blaming or raised voices during the discussion. Nobody wants to feel like they are going to be lectured for 30 minutes or be talked down to. You can bring up experiences if the point is to have a better understanding of each other's points of view, but not to throw a bad choice in someone's face again. Don't have hard conversations when you're hungry, angry, late, lost or tired.

As I discussed earlier in the book, it's important to take a personal inventory to determine what your money beliefs are and how they affect your decisions and relationships. This can be a wonderful time to get to know the person you are going to hopefully spend the rest of your life with. Go through the list of questions and honestly answer them. If you're not open to the answers, the exercise is fruitless…and your money tree likely will be too.

Maybe you've already taken that step and are in a relationship or are married. Maybe you have that blended family where one or each of you has children from a previous relationship. You're in a committed relationship, correct? Okay, so commit to coming together to solve your problems. This takes listening without judgment or negative interpretation, self-assessment and the willingness to change. If you're having trouble coming to a consensus on your own, bring in a third party. This may be a therapist, counselor, member of your religious body or professional advisor.

The adults need to be on the same page and then model togetherness for their children.

I've learned that there is nothing wrong with an adult saying to a child, "I know we used to do things this way in the past, but I've learned some new lessons recently and I believe that we need to do things a little differently for the betterment of our family." It takes swallowing a little pride, but it actually does teach your children about change and that even adults learn new lessons and can change. Instead of digging in your heels and refusing to alter any behavior, you learn and adapt. This helps not only with basic survival, but also with cultivating a happier and healthier family.

Ever meet someone who's living in the past and is grumpy all of the time because things aren't the "way they were back then?" Adaptability is crucial. If things don't bend, over time the pressure will break them. Same goes with relationships. The problem is pride interfering with someone's ability to change and is the culprit for a breakage.

Many of the survey respondents wrote about disagreements between their parents over money. Usually one person was the spender. People responding to the survey are all adults and still have clear memories of their parents' arguments, selfishness with money and rigidity. Did you know that money problems are one of the top reasons people got divorced?

I remember going through a marriage course at our church with my husband called *ReEngage*. The class was a great way to revitalize our marriage after 10 years. We studied 24 traits that strong marriages should have. Every week we discussed another trait, what our current beliefs were and how our individual beliefs may be affecting our relationship. Some people go through the class with little change and blame it on the class, the time commitment or their spouse. My husband and I jumped in with both feet and decided that we needed to do the hard work to honestly look at ourselves, our own beliefs and see how those were affecting our marriage.

You weren't there to throw your spouse under the bus; rather, you had to clean up your own side of the street—you had to examine and change yourself.

What we found was that our beliefs about ourselves, marriage, roles and traits went back to our childhood, as did those of the rest of the class. Trust me, this was a tough experience since we had to uncover some pretty deep and dark parts of our minds and realize that we may have been thinking one way for decades and our perceptions and beliefs were "off" or dead wrong. Once we started to see the world through a different set of lenses, we started to see our marriage shape into what we'd wanted all along. What truly ended up happening was that we came through with renewed strength in our marriage and had learned key tools to keep us on track. One of our motivating forces was this: If we don't examine ourselves and set our lives on a strong path, we were going to pass our baggage along to our daughter.

See, your child sees what you do, hears what you say and watches your actions and body language. That tells the stories that they are going to remember. Your child's belief system is developing from day one, and you're either going to plant good seeds or bad ones. We owed it to our daughter to change, and we owed it to ourselves. This by no means was the easy route, but it was the best route, and the reward is great. Think about this with regard to your financial beliefs and behaviors and how that affects your family. What stories will your children tell themselves based on your family environment? Take the leadership role and do the right thing to help yourself, your children and the future generations. Establish strong roots in your family money tree.

One of the questions I get when either blending families or entering a relationship involves joining the money. You each have preexisting accounts, assets and obligations. Assets that were separate before the relationship should most often remain separate, and attention should be given to those assets to ensure that they are kept legally separate. According to

Brad LaMorgese, Board Certified Family Law Attorney in Dallas, Texas, "An important time to plot out your financial future is if you are asked to sign a prenuptial agreement. Those agreements impact how much support and property you will receive. Can you live on that amount? This is a really important question that must be answered with the help of your financial professional. Why would you unknowingly commit yourself to financial destruction? Most people think their marriage will work, but the fact is, many people who marry get a divorce. Be prepared, not surprised. Always keep track of your money and assets, before you have a problem. Educate yourself about your income, your needs, and your spending. The worst time to try to figure all of that out is in a divorce or family court litigation. If the rainy day has come and you don't know how much money you will need to live your lifestyle, it is probably too late." (LaMorgese)

Make sure to discuss your children and guardianship. If things don't work out, who takes care of your children? Who get the assets? Who controls the decisions? Over the years, I've seen people neglect getting their estate plan together due to indecisiveness with guardianship issues, concern about the cost of the legal work or simply not making the appointment a priority on their calendar. I've found that many people believe that to have an estate plan, you must have a large accumulation of wealth, a large "estate" as in what you may have seen on television or even in neighborhoods around town. An estate plan is simply legally documenting where you want your possessions, your kids and ultimately your own body to go when you are either incapacitated or dead and no longer able to make these decisions. The cost of establishing an estate plan is much cheaper, to set up your documents and accounts properly, than it is to try to clean up a mess in the wake of death or divorce. If you do nothing, your assets and your children may not be cared for properly.

Estate planning is an integral part of a thorough financial plan, cites Catherine Bright, Board Certified Estate Planning Attorney in Dallas,

Texas. "A family's financial plan provides a framework for achieving the financial goals of the family such as buying a home, paying for college and saving for retirement. In short, a financial plan helps the family accumulate and preserve wealth over the lifetimes of family members. The family's estate plan provides a framework for the management and preservation of family assets following the death or incapacity of a family member. The primary focus of the estate plan is on providing financial support for surviving loved ones. An estate plan addresses the important question of what happens to a family's financial resources when a family member dies or becomes incapacitated. Issues of vital importance to the family are addressed in the planning process, including:

- Who will handle the family finances when incapacity or death occurs?

- Who will care for minor children if both parents were to unexpectedly die?

- Who will probate the Will and administer the estate following the death of a family member?

- Who will run the family business following the death or incapacity of the business owner?

- How can any death taxes that will be due be minimized and how will the taxes be paid?

- How will the assets be divided among family members and be accessed by family members for their financial support?

Having an estate plan in place will provide a family with peace of mind that the financial resources accumulated through sound financial planning will be managed and distributed correctly upon the death of a family member. Guardianship decisions can be changed and documents can be amended, so do the planning now and make adjustments down the road as needed. You may change your mind over time as to who you want to raise

your children or who you want to control decisions or who is to receive the assets upon your passing." (Bright)

I know we all hear stories of people passing away unexpectedly and, deep down, we really think that happens to other people. It doesn't. It can happen to you today, so you need to be prepared. Lastly, if you need to do some planning and you've been putting it off, get a good referral and set up an appointment this week to meet within the next couple of weeks. Like I said before, today could be your last.

Earlier this year, I woke up one morning to find that my face felt strangely numb on one side. I looked in the mirror and the entire right side of my face was drooping as if I'd been to the dentist and my eye, cheek, forehead and lip were numb. My heart sank. Here I am getting ready for work, about to take my daughter to school, and I'm seeing in the mirror what looks like a stroke had happened.

Heart disease is in our family, so even though I'm young, it was certainly a possibility. I called my doctor and they got me into their office as quickly as possible. The concern on their faces was instantly obvious. I spent hours in their office doing all kinds of tests. They then came in and said they needed to do an MRI and an MRA of my head and neck to rule out an aneurism or a stroke. The sound of those words twisted my stomach. My daughter is so young and I wanted to see her grow up. I hadn't done all of the things I wanted to do.

I prayed, *God, please don't let it be a stroke or an aneurism.* I vividly remember being placed into the MRA machine and going through the checklist in my head: *Okay, I have my life insurance in order, I have my trust done, I told my daughter and my husband today that I love them...*

Have you experienced this before? I was scared but also relieved at the same time because I had my affairs in order. As it turned out, my droopy face was caused by Bell's Palsy. I recently had a stomach virus, which

happens more often when you have kiddos, and apparently a virus can affect the nerves on your face and cause paralysis or weakness of the muscles. My face returned to normal within a couple of weeks, as did the rest of my life. I was lucky. It could have been something worse. Life can change in an instant, so be as prepared as possible. I've had friends my age who weren't as fortunate as I and now have one parent left to raise the children.

Adding Sunlight

Two realities compelled me to write this book. First off, we owe it to our children to send them out into this world as well-equipped as possible. That doesn't mean our children should be coddled. On the contrary, it means we should take the time to teach them big life lessons. Financial responsibility has to be one of the biggies.

Amazingly so, there are so many young adults that have no concept of money. They use their first paycheck to buy furniture, electronics and stuff for their new place. And they get the full cable package, the latest cell phone and an amazing side effect—a reality check in budgeting, hopefully without 28 percent interest and 5,000 bonus airline miles. Please talk to them about this before it hits them right in the face! Sit down with your child and do a sample budget. Show both wants and needs, but separate them. Show them what they need to bring in every month to pay for what

they need, and then show the *want* number added in. It is a good time to talk about taxes, savings and charity.

The second reality is that I've spoken to hundreds of adults for more than a decade, and so many of them can trace their "money issues" back to their childhood and how money was viewed, used or abused in their family. What I'm asking is that we all take the effort to be frank with our children, and possibly help ourselves as we guide them. It's time to get rid of the excuses and face whatever realities we know we've been trying to hide from and work on them. Check the baggage at the door. Lead by example. Suck it up! Okay, that may have been a little harsh, but the point is clear. Look within and learn and help your children become financially responsible adults. Do the planning for yourself that's needed to get you to where you want to go.

Ever hid your spending from your partner? It happens all the time. I heard one person talk about the fact that they had no idea what they had in their checking or spending account and that they really didn't want to know. They'd rather have their spouse handle it. That's a huge responsibility for the spouse to bear alone. Everyone should have an idea of what they have or don't have. One husband said he knew when his wife didn't want him to know how much she spent on certain grocery items when he opened the refrigerator and the deli stickers were partially torn off where the price was.

There was one day that my dear husband was kind enough to go to the grocery store for me. He stopped off in a specialty grocery store in our neighborhood to pick up a few items. The Sea Bass looked good so he got a couple of fillets for dinner. His intentions were 100 percent positive. To our surprise, the bill was pretty high—thanks to the $40 price tag for two pieces of fish. It was a lovely treat and made for a nice dinner. It did, however, also open up the discussion for us that we needed to check the price per pound at the store before buying something and determine if it was within the budget for a weeknight dinner. We talked and decided we needed to be more aware of the prices and what we wanted to spend for a weeknight entrée. If it was happening all the time, we'd need to decide if that was a value for us and see if we needed to adjust the budget elsewhere. When helping clients with budgeting, I often see cash flow items that will throw the budget off course such as those convenience store drop-ins adding up or larger grocery bills or eating out. Be on the same page with your partner about where the money is going and decide if that is truly where you want to spend your hard-earned cash.

Many families find creative ways to budget. At holidays, drawing names for gifts can lessen the burden for the time shopping, as well as the cost of gift giving. Draw names and have each person give a gift within an established budget for the person they drew. Some families decide not to give gifts all together, but rather all donate to a charity together as a family. Be creative with budgeting and it can be both fun and rewarding.

Start planting good seeds. Your seeds are:

- **Adequate emergency reserves.** Seriously, I don't need to tell you about emergencies. Things just happen. Anyway, have the "cash stash" for those "life learning experiences." Have enough reserves to cover a minimum of six months of living expenses.
- **Next, get the debt paid off.** Ideally, the only debt should be a primary residence first mortgage, and it should be paid off before retirement. Don't incur more debt than you can afford to pay off with one income. If one spouse lost a job, could you afford to stay in the house? For how long? What if it couldn't sell? Maybe you could pay it off sooner and have one less bill when your little ones are in college.

I was so glad that my husband and I paid off his student loans before we had our daughter. We were paying in student loans what a mortgage

payment would be. When the expense of education came along, we had the money since we'd paid off the student and car loans more aggressively when we were DINKS (double income, no kids). We had a mid-sized duplex with handed-down furniture. So many people move into expensive apartments with attractive amenities and fill them with fabulous décor. To ones that could afford it, I say, "salut!" For the others, well, this is for you: "If you can't afford to do it long-term, don't do it." We've just seen the burst of the housing and financial bubbles, and there are thousands of households who can't afford to stay in their house because they bought more than they could afford long-term.

Maybe one spouse had stayed home with the children and the bread-winner lost his or her job. This can happen to a family that was truly living within its means and they just couldn't find employment and over time had to move. Yes, happens all the time. But if we're honest with ourselves, did we really need a house as big as the one we have? Or the car we drive? Or the clothing we wear? We can all cut back places if push comes to shove.

It's truly amazing how cable television is often categorized by people as a *need* rather than a *want*. It's a WANT. So, to get us back on track, we need to get to our needs again and try to get more in check with our goals—life goals, family goals. It is freeing not to be burdened with debt, to know that if push came to shove, you'd be okay for a good while. To me, that's priceless. Take it a step further and teach your children that lesson.

Ashley's Top 15 Financial Seeds to Plant

1. Start contributing at least 10 percent of your gross income to retirement the day you land your first job.

2. You need at least 6 months of liquid (low risk, easily accessible without penalty) emergency reserves in savings.

3. Have your house paid off by the time you retire.

4. Your house payment plus homeowners insurance plus property taxes should not be more than 28 percent of your monthly gross income.

5. Pay your student loans off by the time you retire.

6. Don't put more on a credit card than you can pay off at the end of the month.

7.   Budget 1 percent of your home's value for maintenance (add this to your reserves).

8.   Drive your car as long as possible before getting a new one.

9.   Don't buy something on sale unless you were going to buy it anyway. Otherwise, 50 percent off is still 50 percent more than you needed to spend.

10. Budget: Stick to it and review it at least annually.

11. Comparison-shop rates every year for utilities, phone plans and property, casualty insurance and savings.

12. Once a year, go through your belongings and give to charity what you don't use.

13. Have enough life insurance to meet your family's needs.

14. Talk to your family about each person's long-term care needs and how you are going to handle them as a family.

15. Pull your credit report every year.

Ages and Stages

All children are unique. When teaching your children about money and financial responsibility, ensure that you're tailoring your strategy and lessons to their individual abilities and stage of development. As you and your children go through the various ages and stages of development, keep in mind how you can best communicate with them on their level. Creativity, patience and consistency will be lessons both you and your child will be practicing.

You may have a child with ADHD (Attention Deficit Hyperactivity Disorder) who may struggle with inattention, hyperactivity or impulsivity. Figure out what works best with your child. What are ways to help them remember lessons or tasks? Have a prominent place in the house that lists the rules for allowance, consequences and chores. Help your child organize

and find ways to simplify tasks. Don't neglect teaching your child; rather, teach them in the best way they learn.

Does your child prefer text, numbers or pictures? Is there situational stress in your family? Situational stress could be caused by a divorce, loss of a job or moving schools that emotionally affects child behaviors, so be sure to work with your child to help him or her deal with stress in a healthy way. Knowing your child is part of planting healthy savings seeds in kids. We want the seeds we plant to take root.

Ensure that you don't have any gender bias in your family. Girls need to learn about money and financial matters as equally as, if not more than, their male counterparts. Women, on average, make about 20% less than a man, but expenses may be the same or more than a man's. Unfortunately, over the years I've seen females treated much differently when it comes to financial matters. Just look at some of the investment programs on the television and you may feel like you're watching the NFL draft instead of learning about financial markets. I've had my own business for more than 10 years now, and at dinner parties I still get the question, "Now dear, do you work outside the home?" When we closed on our first house I don't know if the gentleman helping us knew I was even in the room, even though I was the one who calculated all of the numbers and prepared all of the financial documentation.

If you're a statistics person, here are some numbers for you. According to a 2006 Congressional Research Report, women have an average life expectancy of 80.5 years, whereas a man's life expectancy was 75.3 years (Shrestha). Women today make on average 78 percent of the income men make for the same job (Getz). In 2009, median weekly earnings of women who were full-time wage and salary workers was $657, or 80 percent of men's $819 (Labor). Your daughter needs to learn about money and how to make financial decisions. You don't want to teach her to cede financial decisions to someone else because, first of all, there is a likelihood she'll be on her own financially for a portion of her life and secondly, she needs to be aware of how the money in her life works. I've seen many times over the years when either the husband or wife was completely unaware of the financial status of their household. They had no idea where the money was being spent, how much was in savings and retirement accounts or what level of debt they had. In some cases, the spouse found out after a divorce how little they had, even though their family spending gave the illusion of a secure and financially prosperous lifestyle. Don't overlook the need for teaching both boys and girls about money.

Are you a stay-at-home Mom or Dad? You may be relying on someone else for 100 percent of the income in your family. That fact means nothing with regard to your understanding of the family finances. If your spouse does not make it home tonight for whatever reason, you are expected to shoulder the responsibilities moving forward. Do you know what bills you have, to whom you owe money and where your accounts are? If your answer is "No" or "I'm not sure," then find out this week and stay involved.

Teaching Toddlers

Children begin to count somewhere around age 2. Being mindful of choking hazards, give them some play money to count. Use dollar bills or coins and let them count to 10. By touching and feeling the money, they can begin to gain familiarity with currency. You can begin to use the play money for mock scenarios. My daughter has a play shopping cart filled with toy groceries. Decide who's "going shopping" and who's pretending to be the store clerk. Through play, you can show your children how to buy things. "Okay, you wanted to buy the cookies, well, that's two dollars." Show her the transaction between giving the clerk the two dollars and her getting the cookies. You can then go on to show her that she has eight dollars left.

Next time you're out, and you have a have a little cash on you, let your child help you pick something out in the store and then show your child

how you pay cash for the item. They'll remember the time you were play-ing make-believe and will see how it happens in real life, which reinforces the lesson. Better yet, have your child hand over the cash, take the item from the clerk and since I think manners still matter, let him or her say "Thank you" or "Have a good day" to the store clerk. Kids learn from observation and repetition.

So when do you open the dialogue with your kids about money? When they are beginning to be verbal and are able to start repeating words. This is also the time where adults become acutely aware of what phrases and words they use. When my daughter got an exacerbated look on her face and told me that her doll did something *"ridiculous,"* I knew she hadn't picked that up from Sesame Street. Using financial concepts in your daily life will help them gain familiarity with financial words. Their under-standing of the concepts will occur much later, but by introducing the words now, you're building a foundation of knowledge upon which they will build throughout the rest of their lives.

Age 2 begins the "Mine!" stage where it's all about getting what they want. This is a good time to bring home the concept of sharing and giving. Parents who cater too much to the child's material demands will have prob-lems ahead. Patience and love are crucial at this time, as are boundaries. Boundaries set from an early age give both the parent and the child a more solid set of ground rules. Children at this age won't grasp many financial concepts, but take the time to impress the aspects of giving and sharing. When a child is all wrapped up in getting what they want and trying to own everything in the house with the declaration of "Mine!" while grab-bing the object, it creates some perspective when we impress upon the importance of sharing toys and giving some away to others. Toddler lessons should be counting and giving (sharing).

I think back on a time I was on the computer paying bills. My daughter, who was 2 at the time, ran up to me saying, "Mommy, you doing?" Just to clarify that my sentence wasn't a typo, she wasn't saying full sentences yet. If you've had kids that age I'm sure you can remember. So, for me, I was at a decisive point. I could either snap the laptop shut and redirect her attention to something else to avoid the barrage of questions sure to follow, or I could open that can of worms and tell her exactly what I was doing. Thinking back about what my father had done for me, I picked her up, sat her in my lap and stated, "Mommy's paying bills. See how it's light inside the house at night? Well, we use our money so that we can have the lights on. And the food we ate for dinner? Well, we need to pay the grocer for them so I'm telling the bank how much to pay them from our account. Remember when Mommy goes to the bank? Well, we put money in the bank from the money we earn at work and then pay for the things we use."

Just like that! She replied with a little smile and nod, and then just as quickly as she came running up to me, she hopped off my lap and ran off to play. I then took a couple of minutes to finish paying the bills, closed the laptop and proceeded to play with my daughter. Did she grasp it all? Of course not. But children are sponges, and she saw that I was taking the time to pay for things that we use. No need for a big discussion, just very matter-of-fact, like brushing our teeth before bedtime. A child will begin to know that's just part of life. I've known adolescents that still hadn't gotten the grasp of where money comes from and how we pay for things.

It's important not to use any guilt. Saying, "Well, since you wanted swim lessons, we have to try to find money to pay for them," is using guilt. In that case, the parent is trying to place the blame for *their* financial decisions on the child. Be very careful not to put responsibility on the child for your financial decisions. You're the adult and are making the decisions, whether the child is the ultimate beneficiary or not.

As your child enters age 3, their language development starts to pick up. They are not only parroting the words you use but have developed word associations and a clearer understanding of what is actually being

said. Use words such as piggy bank, money, savings and cash. Again, not the time to bring out the *Wall Street Journal* and discuss your portfolio with them (you can start that when they're in high school), but showing cash going into the piggy bank and counting are certainly age-appropriate.

This is also the time where a child starts to develop self-esteem and independence. If you have had a three-year-old in your home, you've prob-ably heard your child say these words, "I am going to do this *all by myself!*" We started hearing that in our home on a daily basis in using the potty, in getting dressed and in playing. At this age, kids are exploring the world and learning their strengths and testing boundaries. Give your child choices and they'll most often give you a clear answer as to what they do or do not want to do, eat, wear, etc. Here is a good time to start to incorporate financial choices.

Here's an example, "Mommy has some money for you to buy a toy. The money can buy one of these two items. Which would you rather have?" Allow your child to pick out what they'd like. Again, your three-year-old is learning self-esteem, so don't criticize or belittle the choice they make. After all, you've picked out the two options for them to begin with. Use patience with them in case they are taking a little time to decide. These are good learning opportunities for parents and children alike!

For Christmas, my husband bought me some "bath bombs", fizzy bath balls that dissolve in the water. I was so excited to use them and knew that they were a special treat since each costs a couple dollars. I let my daughter use one in an evening bath and she was hooked! Each night after, she begged me for another bath bomb to use in her bath. I caved in and let her have one the following night. It then occurred to me that not only were my Christmas presents dwindling down the drain—literally, but my daughter was going through quite a bit of money each night in her bath. The next night when bath time came around, she again begged for the lovely bath bombs. I told her she was more than welcome to have one of the bath bombs but that she'd have to take the cost of the bath bomb out of her piggy bank and buy it from me. She threw a fit at first, but I held firm and told her it was totally up to her, it was her choice. If she wanted the bath bomb she could have it but she was going to have to pay for it. She said she didn't want to use her money so she'd take a bath without it. She had a choice to make and she chose to keep her hard-earned allowance. Kids get these lessons so give them the opportunities for them.

My daughter's introduction to savings was brought on by a cookie. I had gone to our local bakery to pick up a few iced cookies as a special treat. We sat down to have one together. I broke mine in half, placing one on my plate and the other in a container to enjoy later. My daughter looked at me in disbelief and said loudly, "Mommy, what are you *doing?*" I explained how I really loved the cookie, but that I wanted to *save* part of it so I can enjoy some now and the other half later. She understood and smiled, and then said she wanted some of her cookie now and wanted some for later, too. We put her half along with mine, and the next day we were both pleased that the other half of our cookie was saved. We benefitted from a decision made previously. This, in turn, teaches a lesson in cause and effect. Your condition in life is the effect of a multitude of causes, or put differently, the sum of all your choices. Simple savings lessons are all around us. Savings is simply delayed consumption.

Our survey indicated that many parents started talking to their children about money at age 3, while some parents waited until their children were 18 years old. Responses from the parents who cited talking to their three-year-olds about money was quite interesting. One child grasped the concept that if he did chores, he could earn money for things; thus he started doing chores around the house for allowance. Another three-year-old wanted a piggy bank after she realized she had to save her money to be able to buy something. My daughter was given a silver piggy bank when she was born. She loves how shiny it is and loves to pick it up and hear

the coins clank the interior of the pig when she shakes it. We got an inexpensive plastic one as well and let her decorate it with stickers so she could individualize it to make it her own.

The other group of parents who waited to talk with their kids until they were much older struggled with changing bad habits that had already formed in their children and managing expectations. It's like having to pull weeds and replant your yard as opposed to starting with fresh soil, planting good seeds and simple maintenance.

There were many kids ages 4 through 5 who just didn't have much interest in money when their parents talked about it. But around 6 and 7, they started to understand money better and were enthusiastic about earning it and watching it accumulate. Money conversations can start with numbers and counting. Even if saying the words *money, savings* and *allowance* elicits a blank stare, your child, around age 3 or younger, can certainly start off with counting games.

My daughter earned her allowance by feeding our dog and helping out around the house. One day, we planned a trip to the toy store to pick out a birthday present for one of her friends when she very matter-of-factly stated that we were going to have *so much fun* shopping for her friend and that she was getting a new toy too! I told her that she could get a new toy if she liked, but that she was going to pay for it out of the savings from her piggy bank. We sat on the floor and emptied the contents of her cash stash to see what she had saved. Our first lesson was sorting out the various coins into four piles: pennies, nickels, dimes and quarters. Next, we counted together the total number of coins in each category. I showed her how many of each coin it took to equal another. It took five nickels to equal one quarter or twenty five pennies to equal one quarter. She was amazed that the smaller dime was actually worth more than the nickel which was larger in size. We tallied up $7.03 worth of coins in her savings. I told her that there was something called tax that we would have to pay as well, so she could only buy up to $6.45 at the store with her $7.03. Texas sales tax is 8.25%. We filled a small bag with her coins, grabbed her play purse and went shopping. She went all through the store examining everything she could get her hands on. I let her know how much each item was and whether she had enough money or not. It came down to some very difficult decisions. In the end, we came home with stickers, a stamp and some candy. I explained to the store clerk that she had saved up her allowance and was going to pay him herself. This helped establish patience when she handed him her bag of coins. She was so proud of herself and told my husband the second he came home what she bought with *her own money* when we went shopping. I was proud of her that day too!

Reading to your children has numerous benefits in both their vocabulary and brain development. Find some good books and stories that you can read to your children about planning ahead, counting and being prepared. One story I love is the story of *The Three Little Pigs*. Mama Pig sends her three little pigs out into the world with the money they've saved up. The two little pigs that build their houses of straw and twigs lose their homes in a battle with the Big Bad Wolf. The oldest pig saved his money well and built a strong house made of brick. His work ethic, willpower and forethought saved him and his brothers from being conquered by the Big Bad Wolf, and they lived happily ever after. Read this to your child and talk about the story with them. How can this story relate to real life? Which little pig made the best choice? Talk with them about how taking the easy way out can affect them. After hearing this story, my daughter noticed that our home exterior was made of brick, concluding we must have saved well and built a strong house like the third pig had.

Teaching delayed gratification to your children will be an important lesson in life in general, but it will also teach your children quite a bit about money management. Psychologist researcher, Dr. Walter Mischel, conducted a study on children and delayed gratification beginning in the

1960s (Mischel, Shoda and Rodriguez). Four-year-old children were invited into the game room of the Bing Nursery School on Stanford University campus. The classrooms were designed as working laboratories with two-way mirrors. The room was empty except for a chair and a desk. On the desk was a plate filled with various treats such as marshmallows and cookies. He told the children that if they could wait for a few minutes to eat their treat while he stepped out of the room, he would give them a second treat when he returned. Some of the children ate the treat immediately. The second group resisted but didn't wait until he returned, lasting on average three minutes until eating the treat. According to Mischel, about 30 percent of the children were able to wait for the second treat and delay gratification until the researcher returned about 15 minutes later. These children were tempted but found ways to resist such as kicking the table or turning around completely so that the treat was out of sight. (Lehrer, Jonah)

In an article Mischel co-wrote with Yuichi Shoda and Monica Rodriguez, *Delay of Gratification in Children*, they described their finding in following up with those same four year olds. "A recent follow-up study of a sample of these children found that those who had waited longer in this situation at 4 years of age were described more than 10 years later by their parents as adolescents who were more academically and socially competent than their peers and more able to cope with frustration and resist temptation. At statistically significant levels, parents saw these children as more verbally fluent and able to express ideas; they used and responded to reason, were attentive and able to concentrate, to plan, and to think ahead, and were competent and skillful. Likewise they were perceived as able to cope and deal with stress more maturely and seemed more self-assured." (Mischel, Shoda and Rodriguez)

According to Mischel, "What we're really measuring with the marshmallows isn't willpower or self-control. It's much more important than that. This task forces kids to find a way to make the situation work for them. They want the second marshmallow, but how can they get it? We can't control the world, but we can control how we think about it." The skill needed was the "strategic allocation of attention." Instead of obsessing over the marshmallow, children were able to distract themselves to avoid thinking about it. Mischel states, "What's interesting about four-year-olds is that they're just figuring out the rules of thinking. The kids who couldn't delay would often have the rules backwards. They would think that the best way to resist the marshmallow is to stare right at it, to keep a close eye on the goal. But that's a terrible idea. If you do that, you're going to ring the bell before I leave the room. If you can deal with hot emotions, then you can study for the SAT instead of watching television and you can save more money for retirement. It's not just about marshmallows." (Lehrer, Jonah)

Children who had difficulty resisting were shown mental tricks to help them succeed. By pretending the marshmallow was a cloud or a picture in an imaginary frame, children dramatically improved their self-control and were able to wait the full 15 minutes. Mischel says, "Once you realize that willpower is just a matter of learning how to control your attention and thoughts, you can really begin to increase it." He notes that the challenge is turning these tricks into habits, which require years of diligent practice. "This is where your parents are important. Have they established rituals that force you to delay on a daily basis? Do they encourage you to wait? And do they make waiting worthwhile? We should give marshmallows to every kindergartener. We should say, 'You see this marshmallow? You don't have to eat it. You can wait. Here's how.'" (Lehrer, Jonah)

I think back to my savings lesson over my daughter with the cookie. We just need to show them how and incorporate those choices into our daily lives. Proverbs 13:11 *(NIV)*, "Dishonest money dwindles away, but he who gathers money little by little makes it grow."

Teaching your children self-discipline at an early age will help them resist peer pressure, impulse spending and feeling like a failure if instant

success isn't achieved. Parents, and grandparents, can have a hard time saying "No" to their children. Saying "No" doesn't mean you don't love your kids. You love your children enough to say "No" to them. In the long run, your children will understand that they can't get everything they want, which is important both for young children and for adults. A child growing up always getting what they want may have a disappointing adulthood. It's about building some tougher skin. In business, studies show that for every ten prospects you may only get two clients. That's hearing "No" 80 percent of the time. For a child who hears "yes" 80 to 100 percent of the time, the real world can hurt.

Carl Rogers, founder of humanistic psychology, in his book, *On Becoming a Person* (Rogers), writes, "Experience is, for me, the highest authority. The touchstone of validity is my own experience. No other person's ideas, and none of my own ideas, are as authoritative as my experience. It is to experience that I must return again and again, to discover a closer approximation to truth as it is in the process of becoming in me."

In contact sports, the first time you get hit you realize how much it hurts. With practice, you toughen up a bit, both externally and internally, and you figure out the best way to fall or the best way to make impact have the least harm. You practice getting up and finishing the game. There isn't that fear of playing the game because you've gone through the drills in practice. I remember playing softball in high school. We practiced sliding into base. I remember the fear the first time I crashed, not slid, into home base. I got up, dusted the clay colored sand off and got back in line. We had to master the slide and each painful try got a bit easier. In volleyball, we practiced lunging for the ball—rather, strategically sacrificing our bodies so that we came between the floor and the ball in an effort to keep the ball in play. Each try got easier. Come game time, I didn't have to think twice about what I needed to do, it came naturally through practice.

Imagine an NFL team bringing on a linebacker who'd never taken a hit. Is that good or bad for the team? The first time he sees a 220-pound running back headed straight for him do you think he's got his eyes open, in tackle-ready position, ready to take the hit? No, he's probably got one or both eyes closed, ready to fall to avoid being injured. He gets hit and may never want to play again or gets kicked off the team. Ever hear an adult say the phrases, "Life shouldn't be this hard," "I didn't get the deal, so I'm just going to change jobs," "My spouse didn't give me what I want, so I'm moving on?"

"No" means you don't succeed all the time. This is true for life. Children who have been taught this will stay in the game and pick themselves back up when life doesn't go their way. Children who hear "No" for the first time as adults or even adolescents will have a hard time adjusting their expectations. It is perceived as failure instead of feedback and they quit. Developing qualities such as perseverance, persistence, resilience, emotional intelligence and mastery of a skill all come from falling down and getting back up, from practice and from sometimes not getting what we want.

Toddler Seeds

Money Words

Counting

Chores

Role Play

Sharing

Choices

Reading Books With Morals

Planting Preschoolers

A round ages 5 to 6, engage your child in the budgeting process. This is the age where they understand categories and are counting. Budgeting involves three categories: saving, spending and giving. A fun, creative way to start these lessons is to make and decorate containers with labels for their money in three categories such as giving, savings and spending. Decorating containers for their money is a great way to combine creative arts with the beginning of money management and budgeting. The giving jar may have a picture of a church or a local charity or symbols that help them see which bucket the money is going into. The savings jar may have money symbols or a picture of something they are saving for as a goal. The spending jar may have pictures of items they would like to spend their money on. In my daughter's case, that may be a bath bomb or dress-up shoes. Allowance, gifts and working around the community are wonderful

ways for your children to start filling up their containers with money. (See Savings, Spending and Giving Chapter)

My daughter read a book in school by Carol McCloud titled, *Have You Filled a Bucket Today?* (McCloud) Around the house, she'd started using the terms "bucket-filler" and "bucket-dipper", and I was delighted. A bucket-filler is someone who expresses kindness, appreciation and love. A bucket-dipper is someone who is not kind or considerate, "taking" the love from someone else's bucket. This book would be a wonderful supplement to your discussions about giving. How can you be a *bucket-filler* today?

Allowance is a way to teach kids at an early age about working for money. Not every task should come with a bill, but rather talk with your child about specific chores he or she can do and how much you'll pay them for the help. Simply being part of the family shouldn't come with pay. Children ages 5 through 6 should be able to do simple household chores like cleaning their room and making their bed as their responsibility for taking care of their space. Allowance is for something above and beyond that you both have agreed is extra work for some extra cash. Explain how some of their earnings should be set aside in savings for them and another amount should go into charity. Take the time to really explain to them how their $10, with $2 set aside for savings and $1 going to charity is a good thing. This also prepares them for that first real paycheck they bring home that has taxes and benefits taken out. You're setting expectations early on.

Get your child involved in whichever charity or religious organization they'd like to donate to. Letting them pick the charity helps teach them about making decisions, and they'll feel more motivated about giving part of their hard-earned cash for a good cause. This is a good chance to talk about giving in non-monetary ways as well. At least once a year, have your child choose which of his or her toys to give to needy children. This helps de-clutter your home and also helps other families in need. Let your child go with you when delivering the donated toys so that they can see firsthand how great it feels to give. When your kids are older, they can volunteer their time and help the needy. Through this, they gain perspective on the blessings your child has and that it's better to give than to receive.

On December 31st, I decided to finally take our donation bags by our local Goodwill drop-off site with my daughter in tow. I was going start the New Year with a clean guest room. Apparently, December 31st is a busy day to make donations for those trying to get their last charitable donations in for the tax year. There were at least ten cars in line and an extra Goodwill truck ready for the overflow. My daughter said, "Look at all of the other people who are giving their toys, too!" I smiled and agreed how many other people were being bucket-fillers that day.

Let your child be a part of where *your* charitable donations will go for the year. Bringing your child in on the decision-making instills ownership and responsibility. Confirm their ideas and make this a family process. Again, getting them involved where and to whom the money goes does a lot to promote their altruism later in adulthood. As we get older, we all know that everyone needs a little help now and then!

The act of volunteering is far-reaching. You and your child are building a stronger sense of community and awareness of local business as well as the needs of the less fortunate. Charity has a humbling effect on anyone with a sense of entitlement. You're also helping to build social capital. Social capital is value that comes from personal relationships and community involvement. The *Journal of the American Academy of Pediatrics* published a 1998 study (Pediatrics) in which researchers studied the link between social capital and children. There were 667 children, ages 2 to 5, that participated. This was their conclusion:

Our findings suggest that social capital may have an impact on children's well-being as early as the preschool years. In these

years it seems to be the parents' social capital that confers benefits on their offspring, just as children benefit from their parents' financial and human capital. Social capital may be most crucial for families who have fewer financial and educational resources. Our findings suggest that those interested in the healthy development of children, particularly children most at risk for poor developmental outcomes, must search for new and creative ways of supporting interpersonal relationships and strengthening the communities in which families carry out the daily activities of their lives.

There are so many ways to make learning about money fun for the entire family. There is a wonderful board game called, *The Allowance® Game*, by Lakeshore Learning Materials for children ages 5 and up. The board is set up in the *Monopoly* format where each person starts with $3. At each player's turn, they roll the dice and land on a space, such as *Buy Ice Cream-Spend $0.50*, *It's Your Birthday-Receive $5.00* or *Forget Your Homework-Lose Turn*. If you land on the *Bank* space, you have to deposit $2.00 in the bank, and each additional time you land on the bank space, you earn $0.50 in interest. Want to own some property? You can buy a lemonade stand and get paid when other players land on the *Lemonade Stand* space. The first person to earn a total of $20 wins the game. Not only does the game teach the concept of spending, earning money, earning interest and owning a business, it also teaches kids how to make change with the banker and to count. Your child may even find new ways to earn their allowance based on ideas presented in the game.

I was talking with a father the other day when the topic of money and children came up. He recalled going into a store with his six-year-old son where his son immediately wanted a toy he saw. It only cost $3.75, and his son had just glanced at it briefly and immediately wanted it. If you're a parent of a child over age 2, you've been there and know exactly what I'm talking about. So the father reminds his son that he has $5 in his pocket from his allowance and if that's the way he'd like to spend his money he can, but that he needs to know he'll only have $1.25 left. The son proceeded to pick up the toy and look it over from every angle, as if examining its worth. After a minute of this, he set the toy down and agreed to come back and make the decision before they left the store. Guess what the six-year-old did? When they came back by the toy, he told his dad that he'd rather wait because he wanted to save his $5 for something else.

I love this. The father gave his child the *ability to make a financial decision* and *supported* the decision the child made. He's building confidence and financial awareness at such an impressionable age. We need to think about all of the times we have these learning opportunities with our children. Take the time now; it will pay dividends later.

A friend of mine had a great idea when it came to Halloween. In teaching our children about boundaries and limits, where does the huge bag of Halloween candy come into play? Granted, we all enjoy a little Halloween candy now and then, but ask my dentist friends about the havoc that it can wreak on children's teeth and you may want to stop your kids from eating the entire bag. In my friend's family, they use the concept of the *Switch Witch*. Each child can pick out a certain number of pieces of candy, and the rest goes on the front porch for the *Switch Witch*. The *Switch Witch* comes the day after Halloween and switches out the bag of candy for a toy, game or book.

A second option would be to donate the candy to organizations such as Operation Gratitude, which sends care packages to the military troops overseas. Many local dentists have organized Candy Buy-Back programs that offer incentives such as paying $1 per pound of candy donated. The dental office will then take on the responsibility of coordinating delivery of the care packages. Your family would have helped another and your child

would have earned a little money in the process, in addition to possibly saving money on future dental bills.

Starting around age 5, set up monthly family meetings. Family meetings are scheduled, sacred times for your family to meet to talk about what's going on at school, at work and any changes that may be ahead for your family. I understand that schedules can get busy and things can pop up that try to interfere, but be consistent and stick to the scheduled meeting, regardless of how hectic your life becomes. You're letting your child know that there is a set time every month that the family comes together to talk about the family. This may be a time for you to talk about and plan ahead for a vacation or bring up an extracurricular activity that needs to be addressed (and budgeted for).

For older children, the agenda should include your child's savings. Review monthly what your child has saved. Talk with them about a goal they have and the dollar amount of that goal. For younger children, it could be a toy or maybe a video game. For an older child, it could be a phone or school trip. Family meetings are a place where your child gets to talk about their feelings and thoughts, where you show your child that it's safe to come to you and where you reinforce that it's important for you to communicate as a family.

Make sure everyone understands that what is discussed in the family meeting stays in the meeting. Be sure to keep the discussions age-appropriate so they don't get confused or feel that their life as they know it is coming to an end. Your child's understanding of what's going on inside the family will help them understand why you may say "No" to a *want* they have. Otherwise, they may feel that they're being punished for something and won't know why. For example, if a parent loses a job, the family may need to change their spending habits. If explained in a way that brings the family together, the child may not feel rejected if they are unable to do something they used to. It can be a way to have the family put all of their heads together to find ways that everyone is working together to save money.

For older children, help them figure out how much they need to save to pay for what they want. If the item is pricey they need to understand the time and work it will take to reach that goal. If they aren't able to accumulate that amount by chores around the house (because you're not the bank after all), help them find other ways to earn the money. Otherwise, they may need to revisit the goal later. You may agree to match their savings once they reach a certain goal. You want them to succeed but don't want to simply hand over the farm.

As a parent, the important lessons you're teaching your children will be endless. Teaching a child to work for their goals, save money, give to charity and be creative last a lifetime. Simply by giving your child the toys they want without effort on their part is instilling entitlement in your child. Have your child start a list of all their wants so they can possibly consider those for birthdays and holidays. Often, by the time the birthday or holiday comes around, they really don't want the same things anyway.

The Neuropsychology of Self-Discipline, (SyberVision Systems), teaches a process for setting and working toward goals. What is the goal? Start with a defined purpose. What do you want to achieve? Is it possible? Find role models who have achieved those goals as a way to motivate. What does it *feel* like? Tune into what it feels like, not what it looks like. Let's assume your child wants a bike. Have them describe how it feels to ride the bike. Do they feel energized with the wind blowing in their hair? Just picturing yourself on the bike has a very different feeling. Really feel what it's like to achieve the goal. For adults, picture how it *feels* to be retired? Are you relaxing on a comfortable couch reading a book on a rainy day, with the aroma of homemade soup wafting through the air? Are you at peace? Maybe you feel the sting in your hands of hitting the golf ball on a warm

sunny day and can smell the freshly cut greens. Putting yourself in that place and feeling it will impact your success.

Now take the feeling you just had of being on the golf course or relaxing reading a book and keep that emotion present as your new passion and motivation. You're lighting that fire to keep the goal alive. Next, what's your plan for reaching the goal? You want to achieve it, so now determine which steps to take. Your vision is now a plan. What skill set or education do you now need to implement the plan? Knowledge leads to confidence, and confidence gives you the drive to succeed. Persistence keeps you on track, and perseverance keeps you going in face of adversity.

What if your child comes to you and wants to be a doctor some day? Find some doctors that he or she can meet and talk to. Maybe your child can shadow the doctor at their office for a day. Better yet, see if they can stay in touch as he or she works toward the goal to help motivate. What does it feel like to be a doctor? How do they feel helping people get well? What steps do they need to take to become a doctor? With each step they build confidence and they get closer to their goal. What education, skills and resources do they need? Are they determined to succeed no matter what? How do they stay on track when life pushes them off course? Their goal may be to graduate from high school. Help them through the process and encourage them.

Peer pressure is becoming more prevalent during this time. Make sure your child is hearing what *you* have to say, not just what their friends are saying. You may start to see more pressure to buy certain items or go to certain events. Know what messages your child is receiving so you know what to work with. Your family meeting will help ensure everyone is on the same page and that everyone feels valued. Listen to your child about what's going on at school and any struggles or questions he or she may be having about life. As adults, you can be there for guidance and planning. After all, you're on the same team.

The one quality which sets one man apart from another—the key which lifts one to every aspiration while others are caught up in the mire of mediocrity—is not talent, formal education nor intellectual brightness—it is self-discipline. With self-discipline, all things are possible. Without it, even the simplest goal can seem like the impossible dream.

—Theodore Roosevelt

Preschool Seeds

Delayed Gratification

Money Containers: Saving, Spending and Giving

Allowance

Social Capital

Money Games

Family Meetings

Caring For Our "Other Children"

Iwill first start by saying that I am a pet and animal lover and have always had a pet in my house. I believe they offer great companionship and are our best buddies. I will also admit that I've spent thousands of dollars on pets over the years. Our English Springer Spaniel, pictured above, is our latest rescue dog. I just could not imagine our family without him. He's also a line item on our budget, listed as *Pet Care*. You need to keep track of how much you're spending on food, veterinary visits, vaccinations, preventative medications, treats, doggy daycare, grooming and so on. It adds up quickly. Our dog needs his monthly groom or his hair gets matted, and we're responsible pet owners so we keep him properly groomed, vaccinated and cared for. I remember coming home from work one afternoon and he had thrown up all over the living room. Just looking at him, I knew he needed to go to the vet. Since it was after 5 p.m. and our

veterinarian's office was closed, our only option was the emergency animal clinic. I loaded him into the car and took him in. After many tests and $300 later, he just had really bad case of an upset stomach. I was able to wash and clean the furniture so I saved the upholstery cleaning bill, but we've had to do that in the past, and upholstery and carpet cleaning can be costly!

Coco was another canine love of mine. I was running home to let her out before a dinner party and decided to throw the tennis ball for a quick game of fetch. After all, I was being a dutiful pet owner and playing with her and giving her exercise. She jumped up to get the tennis ball, a beautiful leap by the way, and landed on some metal edging in our yard. Blood started gushing from her foot, and I quickly saw the gash. Luckily the vet was open until 6 p.m. that night, so we were able to forgo the emergency animal clinic charge, but the stitches and shot ran us a couple of hundred dollars regardless.

Now, again, let me remind you that *I am an animal lover* and have rescued many animals. Just know what you're getting into in being a pet owner and plan it in your budget. Be sure to take this into consideration when you're choosing to get a pet. Will it need training? Will you need someone to help let it out when you're at work? What is the typical maintenance for your pet? When your little one wants to adopt *another* puppy or the neighbor's cat had a litter of kittens, go to the budget and see if you can afford the pet and the maintenance first. If not, you'll feel bad for about 10 minutes and then move on. Hey, you've at least got your one buddy. I've seen families spending thousands of dollars on pets and couldn't figure out why they couldn't save for retirement or put money away for their kid's college. It's all about choices. When your child is older and responsible enough to help care for a pet, you can have them use part of their allowance to pay for the dog food or vet visits. A child will learn that pets are a big responsibility and that part of that responsibility is being able to provide for them. Just like you provide for your child, having their furry friend is worth giving up some of their allowance and time needed to train, walk and care for their pet.

Seedlings in School

Your little one is now entering first grade. They will be exposed to a whole new world. At home, integrate math and money lessons to strengthen both areas while making them more relevant. When studying addition and subtraction use real money to illustrate the concepts. Role-play is a wonderful bonding experience, but it's also good exposure to a real-world situation. Start with ten $1 bills. Have a list of items to buy with a price attached, or take some items from your house and put price tags on them. Let them pick what they would want to buy with their ten dollars. Make sure they have both higher and lower-priced options. We're going to start off assuming tax is included in the prices. Did they pick the $8 toy and only have $2 left? How many items could they buy? Next, let them be the cashier and have them make change for your purchases.

If your child is multiplying and dividing, you can see how many $2 items their $10 will buy. Let's say your child gets $5 per week in allowance.

How long will it take him to save up for that $10 toy? Ten dollars divided by $5 per week is 2 weeks. Maybe your child likes the really big-ticket items and wants something that costs $100. Show them how $100 divided by $5 is 20 weeks. There are 4 weeks in a month, so 20 divided by 4 is 5 months of allowance to save up.

Teach your children to budget and comparison-shop. The next time you're at the store, make a fun game of allowing your child to do some of the shopping. Let them have a few dollars as their budget to shop for certain items. Teach them to comparison-shop for each item and add up the total for their purchase. Maybe their list includes yogurt, milk and cereal and you've budgeted a certain dollar amount for those items. They must get all the items on their list and stay within the dollar amount given. Show them the difference between items on sale and full-priced items. Maybe they can find a coupon to help the money go a little further.

Another activity that would help parents and children alike would be to help you get organized. Your child could earn some extra spending money by helping you shred papers to de-clutter your home office or even your business files if you're self employed. Your kids are able at this age to help file, assemble mailings and organize those piles that may have been forever on your to-do list. Around the holidays, they can help send out holiday cards, wrap gifts and plan meals. Think of all of those things that take up your time. See if they'd like to assist you and earn some additional allowance or earn privileges in the process.

Seeds In School

Math
Role Play
Real World Scenarios

Growing Up

Adolescence can be a very challenging time for both children and adults, but it's also a wonderful time to see your children bloom. You've planted healthy seeds in your children and they have been germinating in them for some time. It's time for those seeds to really take root so they can grow. This can be a time during which a great shift occurs. Parents may start to see power struggles and peer-pressure increase, not to mention puberty. Ensure your child is aware of family rules and consequences. Family meetings are very important during this time, so you'll be glad you started this tradition years ago. If your child is expecting a car when they turn 16, this may be a good time to discuss budgeting and show your child what they would need to save for that goal. Set the expectations early on to avoid some conflicts down the road.

Dr. Andrew McGarrahan, a child psychologist in Dallas, Texas, works with children ranging from age 8 to young adults in their 20s. According to Dr. McGarrahan, around middle school is the time when children may no longer do things just to please you. They feel more grown up and are more apt to work for incentives than their earlier desire just to please you. They need to be responsible around the house, for example, cleaning their room and taking out the trash, as part of being in the family. Incentives are a way for your children to earn an allowance for doing something extra, and above and beyond what's already expected.

Parents and children need to work together to arrive at what the incentive is and how it is earned. Talk to your child about what motivates them, what they want to work for, so that the incentive really does drive them. As a parent, you want them to get the reward and to succeed. Be clear about how they earn the incentive and when they receive it. Video games tend to be the activity of choice for this age group. Allow your children to be incentivized so if they do some additional chore, like helping in the yard or around the house, you would in return give them money for a video game. For younger children, they may choose stickers or a smaller reward for their work. According to Dr. McGarrahan, it's important to make sure that the incentive, the video game, is something that they buy for themselves—not something you would normally give. It needs to be that special thing they've earned for themselves. Instead of buying the item for them once they've saved enough money, take them to the store, have them pick out what they want and have them pay for it out of their own pocket. (McGarrahan)

Engage them in the process. If they want something a bit more expensive, you may make an agreement to match a portion of the money they've saved once they reach a certain dollar goal. This is a real-world lesson in saving for a goal. By matching a portion, you are exposing them to what it may be like if an employer matches a retirement plan contribution or to

have a job with an incentive for a bonus. This early exposure plants seeds that add to the myriads of other tidbits of information that sharpen someone's financial knowledge.

As your children get older, allowance alone may not be what it takes to motivate them. Privileges may be a way to do just that. You may allow them the privilege of computer time once they've completed their homework. Other ideas could be allowing them to pick out what to have for dinner or what movie to rent for Friday night. Again, make sure the incentive is something your child actually wants. Otherwise, they probably won't stick to it for long. Similarly, the lack of doing homework may mean a privilege is taken away. Be specific and clear with your child about the rules, and be consistent with enforcing them.

Growing Seeds

Incentives
Increased Responsibilities

Teaching Teens

Slowly add responsibilities. Here's the conundrum: We want to shape our children to be responsible adults. That means we have to start giving them responsibilities, which can be hard for parents to do. We remember too well holding them in our arms, changing diapers, watching those first steps and hearing their first words. The time seems as though it has just flown by and suddenly our kids are young adults. It's our responsibility to teach them about things like credit and savings and car insurance. They grow up in a flash and you realize they are either going to learn (the correct) lessons from you or they are going to learn (maybe not so correct) lessons somewhere else. Here is your quest! I won't subject you to the Monty Python Quest scenario, figuring the air speed velocity of the African Swallow.... You get something more down-to-earth. **Do the very best you can, educate *yourself* and lead by example.** I can bet that you will end up in a better place and you and your child will have shared a

wonderful experience. So, you're going to have to start giving your child opportunities to be responsible.

Starting around the teenage years, you may want to convert their savings and spending jars into checking and savings accounts. You can deposit their allowance and their hard-earned income into an account and give them a debit card for their spending. At this age, they are able to categorize the transactions and, with your help, keep track of expenses and deposits. They are still influenced by their parents and are still a little shy of the phase where they think they know everything. These can be great times for character building, solidifying self-confidence and understanding humility.

Take your child to the bank with you. Are you scared yet? It's a good idea if you can get them to go inside so they can see it's a real place and not just a window where you drive up to hand over money—they may confuse it for a fast food restaurant. Let your child know that you are putting their allowance in the bank to save for later. You can let your child know that the bank is keeping it in a safe place for you until you need it and while it's staying in there, it's growing. If your child has worked and earned money, help them to deposit that money into the account. They'll feel better knowing their money is in the same place as yours. If you're paid direct deposit like most people now, you can still do the same exercise by a deposit from a gift or just to put some money in their account.

When discussing savings with your child, be sure to mention interest. You might demonstrate this by having your child plant a seed or a small plant and leaving it on the windowsill. Like money, the growth is slow, but steady. You could also use any number of software programs that can show the growth in a graph format. Print the graphs and put them on the refrigerator. A child loves the fact that they can put their money somewhere safe and watch it grow! Sam Wyly, a self-made billionaire, recalls his first lesson in earning interest. His mother opened a bank account for him

at age seven and deposited a few dollars. The goal was to use that money for college. Sam learned, "If I put money into the account on a regular basis, it would grow in two ways. One, by sheer fact that I was saving it rather than spending it on Cokes and movies; and, two, because the bank would be paying me to keep my money there. I figured out for myself a third benefit: the more I put into the account, the more I'd get from the bank." (Wyly 2)

Ask them what they want to save for so they can get excited about reaching their goal. Maybe they want a toy or a big birthday party, and they want to save up their money to get it. You can find easy financial calculators online or in most computer programs in standard operating systems. If your child is more right brained, print out a graph showing their accumulated savings and their target. Help your child calculate how much they'll need to save. You may even offer to contribute or match once they reach a certain level (I don't recommend matching for each dollar, rather once they've reached a goal). Saving is a good self-confidence lesson. They need to know they can do it on their own and they should take pride in their accomplishment. Confidence comes from working toward something you want and earning the money to pay for it.

I think of the times when I've stepped back and allowed my daughter to do something on her own that I had normally done for her or helped her with. Resisting the urge to jump in and help, I watched her work through the problem on her own. I could clearly hear the excitement and pride in her voice when she cheered, "I did it!" We don't like to use the word "can't" in our family. Anytime we hear our daughter saying, "I can't do it," we make sure she's actually tried to do it on her own first and if she has, then we ask her to rephrase her statement as a request for help. Help is not doing it for someone; help is teamwork.

When you feel that your child is ready, begin putting their allowance on a prepaid debit card; this will help your child learn about spending

using something other than cash. It is important to first talk with your bank about the debit card parameters. Make sure the bank will only allow purchases up to the amount on the card. Some banks will allow for a certain dollar amount over your balance, but will in turn charge a hefty overdraft fee. Federal regulations now require that customers have the choice whether to opt in to get overdraft protection on their account. If you opt in and exceed your balance the card company will allow the charge but will charge you a bank overdraft fee.

Here's why you may want to opt *out*. You put $50 on the debit card and specify to your child what purchases can be used on the card. Say your child is just learning some financial lessons and buys a $48 dollar item thinking they fall within the $50 limit. In Texas, our state sales tax is 8.25 percent. That $48 item hits the card for $51.96. Your child is $1.96 over the limit and gets charged a $35 overdraft fee. Ouch! If you opt out, the merchant will decline the purchase and save you and your child the overdraft fee. Maybe this is a good way for your child to start learning how taxes come into the picture, as well as a lesson in rejection. If the merchant leans over the counter and says to your young financial protégé, "I'm sorry, but your card is *declined*," that can make a lasting impression: Stay within budget and make room for taxes.

Debit cards are great ways to allow parents to give a specified amount of money to their children, to teach responsibility and to allow parents *and* kiddos to keep track of where the money is going. This is a good start in budgeting for you and your children. Many full-service gas stations have food, even a restaurant attached, where added expenses come in (food, drinks, etc). Have a child over the drinking age? You don't want your gas card being used to buy their college buddies beer! Set a meeting and discuss the parameters of the card. What can it be used for, and what is off limits? Discuss what constitutes an emergency (an emergency is not a denim sale).

Parents should have online access to the account to be able to view at any time what the card was used for. In your monthly meeting, review the account to see what was purchased and talk about any experiences, positive or negative, that you or your child had with using it. Take the time to discuss how much of the expenses were in each category such as food or gas. Your child is learning to shop responsibly under your careful supervision and learning valuable lessons on cash flow. It's either going to be you or the college roommate who's going to influence your child's first actions with debit/credit. Hmmm…I choose the parents.

Think of teaching credit along with teaching credibility. Credibility (credit) is needed in life. It takes a long time to build and seconds to destroy. Credit in essence means you're good for it. The next time you buy something on credit, ask yourself, *Am I good for it? Can I pay for this?* Credit card spending limits are assessed based on income, debt and credit history. The card should be for specific purchases that you can monitor. Your child making smart choices with credit is so important. Talk about what goes on the card and what the child's limits are. You'll need to set expectations for usage, payments and consequences for misuse.

Now take a little time to think about *your* spending. Do you use a list when shopping or do you impulse buy? Are you always returning items to the store with buyer's remorse? Are there things in your house or closet (or child's closet) that have never been or have rarely been used? Be sure to work on your own habits to better show your children how to spend. Think about holidays and special occasions. Do you feel sick from your credit card bill after the holidays? I've seen families that spend thousands of dollars on the kids during the holidays, yet don't think they'll have enough money for stated goals. Smart shopping and setting limits is good for both you and your kids.

As parents, we take on the responsibility of raising our children to be the best adults they can be and have the responsibility to plant healthy seeds. Once they graduate from high school they should be able to do certain tasks and take on certain responsibilities. I almost hesitate to write

this but it needs to be said. In my view, the list should include some very obvious lessons in general and I feel obligated in writing this book to mention. Truth be told, there are too many adults that struggle with the basics:

- Wardrobe: Yes, be able to dress yourself. This is not always obvious if you've ever walked on a college campus. Be able to pay for the basics and save up for the wants. I understand some kids like to buy expensive clothes, but they need to have a way to pay for them on their own some day.
- Cooking: Even if it means putting frozen chicken in the oven, your child should know how to feed themselves without having to go to a restaurant and pay for take out or dining in.
- Laundry: Washing clothes and sheets will come in handy. If you've always done the wash or had a house keeper, teach them to do their own laundry by the time they leave your home.
- Studies such as reading, writing and mathematics, hopefully learned by high school graduation. Math skills strengthen financial skills. Otherwise, it's up to you to teach them.

Now, I've met some adults that lack full capacity in these areas, but parents, please help get your children ready. Now let's layer on some additional financial necessities:

- Balancing a check book every month. Key word is **balance.**
- Stick to a budget and live within **your** means.
- Use credit to build history but pay off the balance every month.
- Pay bills on time.
- Make phone calls to providers to discuss your accounts and negotiate fees, limits and options. This skill comes in handy during a dispute or inquiry. It is also a good lesson in healthy conflict resolution.

Charles Schwab conducted a survey in 2010 called *Insights into Money Attitudes, Behaviors and Concerns of the Sandwich Generation* (Schwab)). The study revealed that 41 percent of the respondents still provide some level of financial support to their children ages 23 through 28. Of those, only half say their children are mostly independent, 35 percent expect their kids to achieve independence by age 30, 8 percent by age 35, 2 percent by age 40 and 4 percent say, "Never." As for the parents, their stated priorities were *saving for retirement* for 56 percent of the respondents, and 44 percent said *helping their children financially* was a priority.

So are these parents financially set, and do they have the ability to help pay for their adult children? Not in their minds. Of them, 29 percent worried about not being able to retire, 22 percent worried about outliving retirement money and 22 percent worried they weren't saving enough. We need to be better about equipping our children with the skills and resources to be able to provide for themselves—hence the word *independence*. In *my* survey, I asked whether the respondents rely on someone else for financial support. Of the respondents, 24 percent indicated they did rely on someone else for financial support, and 35 percent indicated they were expecting an inheritance. If your children are able to provide for themselves, they aren't relying on you, which allows you to save for your own retirement, put money in savings and lessens the worry of outliving your money.

Saying "No" to your adult children could be one of the best lessons for them. Once they start to rely on themselves, their confidence, independence and maturity grows. Just be willing to set the boundaries and see it through. In the Schwab study, 64 percent believed their kids are not worried about being a financial burden on them, and 20 percent of the respondents believe that twenty-somethings have more of a sense of entitlement to money than previous generations. What do you think contributed to that sense of entitlement? Were they given things, or did they have to work for them? Were they sheltered from financial

discussions or brought into the talks? Were they bailed out when they made a mistake, or did they assume responsibility and pay the consequences? One-fourth of the respondents cited overspending was cause of their reliance on their parents, and 19 percent cited consumer debt. Looking at their own children, the parents' top financial concerns for their kids were not saving enough for retirement, emergencies and having too much credit card debt.

It is crucial to talk to your child, especially your teenager, about the time value of money. If they're going to take any business classes in college, they'll have a leg up from learning this from you. The time value of money is the idea that a dollar today is worth more than a dollar in the future, because the dollar received today can earn interest up until the time the future dollar is received. It not only applies to earning interest; it applies to interest you're paying! You put $100 dollars on the credit card that charges you 20 percent interest annually, and at the end of the year you *owe* $120! Maybe you decided to save the money and earn 5 percent and now *have* $105. Instead of interest, what if that annual rate referred to the inflation rate, what the change in the purchase price would be? If the cost of goods went up by 3 percent per year, the $100 item today may cost you $103 in a year.

This is a good time to talk about paying for college. Let's assume you only need $8,000 per year for tuition, but you are offered $10,000 per year in student loans with an 8 percent interest rate. Your new college student thinks, *Hey, a little spending money wouldn't hurt! After all, I don't have to start paying it off until I graduate, and by then I'll be making good money!* What does that decision cost?

Let's assume you took the Master's degree route and graduated in 5 years, with a $10,000 loan per year, for a total of $50,000 in student loans with repayment deferred until graduation, but interest beginning when you took the loan. Upon graduation, you would owe approximately

$63,360 for the $50,000 in loans you accepted. Assume the terms of this loan allow you *up to 25* years from graduation to pay back the debt in full. If you take the 25 year repayment schedule, you would pay a monthly payment of approximately $485 per month on the loan. The total ***interest*** paid on the $50,000 loan would be around $95,735, nearly twice the amount of money you borrowed. If you accelerated your payments and paid your loan off in 10 years instead of the 25 years, your monthly payment would have been higher at roughly $764, but you your total interest paid on the loan would be closer to $41,637, about $54,000 less than the 25 year repayment plan!

What if you only took what you needed and borrowed $8,000 per year instead of $10,000 per year? Your student loan balance would be around $50,690 at graduation. Taking the 25 year repayment plan, your total interest paid would have been around $76,500, paying $390 per month. Lessoning that to 10 years would be closer to $33,250, paying $610 per month in payments.

Assumes 8% interest beginning at loan inception and payment deferral until graduation.

			Cost of Taking Additional	
Loan Each Year for 5 Years	$ 8,000	$ 10,000	$2,000	
Loan Balance at Graduation	$ 50,690	$ 63,360	$	12,670
Paying Loan off 25 Years from Graduation				
Monthly Payment for 25 Years	$ 390	$ 485	$	95
Total Interest Paid	$ 76,500	$ 95,735	$	19,235
Total Principal and Interst Paid	$ 116,500	$ 145,735	$	29,235
Paying Loan off 10Years from Graduation				
			$	
Monthly Payment for 10 Years	$ 610	$ 765	155	
Total Interest Paid	$ 33,315	$ 41,640	$	8,325
Total Principal and Interst Paid	$ 73,315	$ 91,640	$	18,325
Difference Between 10 Yr and 25 Yr Payoff	$ 43,185	$ 54,095	$	10,910
Cost of Taking Additional $2,000				
***and* Paying over 25 years instad of 10 years**	$		**72,420**	

That extra "spending money" or "fun money," or whatever you call it, in this case cost you quite a bit of money. It's good to have the financial data in front of us so we can make some educated decisions. I think if

more people knew how to use some of these basic financial calculators, they would take a little extra care with their financial decisions.

When buying a house, think what the true long-term cost of the mortgage will mean. Maybe you qualify for a loan up to $500,000 but, from a cash flow perspective, the $300,000 house is more in your price range. What if you bought the more expensive house, since, after all, you did qualify for it and it has all the latest amenities? That extra $200,000 as a 30-year mortgage at 5 percent interest costs you over $186,000 in interest. Buying the $500,000 home really cost you $686,000 long term. You can find free mortgage calculators online as well as amortization schedules that will tell you what the total interest would be. Most calculators have an extra section where you can see what the overall impact of paying a little extra every month would be. A little extra payment on a loan will not only take off interest paid over the loan; it will also shave off time!

Teen Seeds

Bank Accounts

Debit

Credit

Budgeting

Privileges

Planting Inside The Perimeters

Charles J. Sykes, in his book, *Dumbing Down Our Kids* (Sykes), goes into some pretty great rules that I believe are important to share with your pre-teen or teenager. He starts off with rule No. 1: "Life is not fair. Get used to it." Rule No. 15, in addition to all of them, is great to share with your child. It says, "Flipping burgers in not beneath your dignity. Your grandparents had a different word for burger flipping. The called it 'opportunity.'"

Discussing expectations of what comes after your kids leave your care is truly important. Expectations come from family, other relationships and society. Problems arise when you're unaware of the expectations and when the expectations are unreasonable. You need to be clear about when your financial support ends, whether moving back home after graduation is an option or not, and what your child should expect from an employer. How

you become clear is communicating openly and honestly about your expectations and discussing the expectations of your child.

The expectations your children have should be in line with their reality. If you've financially supported your children through high school, but you're cutting the cord upon graduation, please communicate that with them. What are your expectations of your children and what are their expectations of you? If you don't communicate and expectations are not met, this can lead to sadness, disappointment, frustration and anger.

Have a budget discussion with your child *before* they go off to college to ensure everyone is on the same page. I spoke to a group of high school seniors about five months before their graduation. Not one person had sat down with their parents and discussed budgeting and what level, if any, financial support their parents would provide for their education. Sit down with your child before they leave for college and do the budget.

Discussion Points:

- If your child decides to spend eight years getting an undergraduate degree, does that mean you're still footing the bill?
- Are you going to cover graduate courses?
- How about room and board? Social organizations?
- Can they move home after graduation or do they need to get their own place to live?
- What expenses are you going to pay for and what's the budgeted amount?
- What do they need their own money to pay for?

Your child needs to know if they are going to be paying for some or most of the expenses so they can plan ahead. This also helps you. When the expectations are clear from the beginning, you may avoid some of the calls from your college student asking for extra money.

Sample College Budget Worksheet

Income	Monthly	Annually
Employment Income		
Money From Parents		
Gifts Received		
Other Income		
Total Income		

Expenses	Monthly	Annually
Bank fees		
Books		
Cable		
Car loan		
Car insurance		
Clothing		
Clubs		
Eating Out		
Entertainment		
Fuel		
Gifts		
Housing		
Internet		
Maintenance		
Personal Care		
Phone		
Savings		
School Fees		
Spending Cash		
Tuition		
Utilities		
Other		
Total Expenses		
Total Income Less Total Expenses		

My parents paid for my tuition, books and fees directly to the university. They then gave me a set amount of money that was to cover everything else: apartment, food, utilities, sorority, etc. I worked during the summer and on breaks for some additional money. I wanted to be an adult, so I felt I needed to start pitching in a bit more and doing my part.

Parents who continue paying for grown adult's expenses are sending unintended messages. You may be just trying to help out here and there or have agreed to keep funding car insurance or another bill. In doing so, your adult child may feel that there will always be a safety net, a lifeline, to fall back on and may never truly feel they need to be 100 percent responsible for themselves. Another issue stemming from continuing to support financially dependent adults is the resulting inability to fund your own goals.

If the cut-off date is fixed and unemotional, the child doesn't feel like your love is being shut off, rather just your bank account. Hopefully you've done a good enough job raising them thus far so that money is not tied to love in the first place. If you are set financially and want to do some giving, you may want to have discretionary gifts as part of your estate planning or help pay for the grandkids' education. These strategies send a different message than the message of parents being the backup plan.

The Importance of Edging

Your goal, I'm sure, is to show your child love and to provide them with what they need. Always funding your child's wants, however, sends the message that in order to be happy, they must have possessions. Maybe it starts off with a toy and then the iPhone, next the new car and the flat screen TV. I've seen a grown man go home from work with a new $70,000 car just because he wanted it. First of all, where was the communication with his spouse regarding such a purchase? Secondly, why such an impulse purchase? His reasoning was that he felt he had worked hard, that it was "his money" to spend how he wanted, regardless of how his wife felt since he worked and she didn't, and he just deserved it for being him. See any money issues here? What message was that sending to the kids? Earlier that day, he may have taught his kids some important lesson about money, but what do you think the kids learned? They see that Daddy is so successful that he gets fun toys. They want to be like that when they

grow up, which means buying fun toys too as either a reward or just being alive. In the meantime, Mom's upset and the kids don't know why or she complains to the kids, who in turn learn that money is something to fight over. Again, what message is being sent to the kids? It's *not* about what you tell them; it's the *actions* that make a lasting impression.

Gosh, these kids are off to a great start in life! My point is this: Think about what money messages you're sending your kids. Children pick up on so many nonverbal cues, which start shaping who they are going to be, what beliefs they have and what money means to them. First, figure out what it means to you and what messages you've been sending. It's never too late to make it right. In fact, talk with your kids about it. "Hey, I realized that I made a mistake when I bought something. I think I was feeling ____ and bought something to feel better. I shouldn't have done that. What I should have done is ____." It's a hard day when we show our children that we're not perfect. But honestly, it's better for everyone. You will start learning more about yourself, and your child will see that if you make a mistake you should learn from it and get past it. Perfection isn't the goal; the goal is being a better parent and a good leader for your family.

In our survey, we asked people to describe a memory from childhood that made an impact on their financial lives. I want to share some of those stories with you.

When my dad lost his job when I was in high school, I remember thinking that I needed to save money in case that ever happened to me. But then I did not notice a big change in our lifestyle, so I forgot that saving money lesson, and I think learned instead that somehow everything works out financially. That is a misconception that I periodically deal with in my own life and is something I have to remind myself of so I do not get into financial trouble.

Hah! If you only knew... My favorite memory... getting injured (accidentally) by my father and him having to take me to the emergency room for stitches. After we got home he was so upset and felt so guilty and didn't know how to make me feel better so he gave me $100. That's how it worked in my house. Money solved emotional problems. If my parents fought, my mom shopped. If you were down and needed to be cheered up, a shopping trip or cash payment was just the fix.

When I learned that the Slurpees I had after elementary school were $1 each, I learned the value of a dollar. When my mom offered me $5 to fold laundry—Wow!—that was 5 Slurpees! When I could buy a necklace for $30, I had to determine whether that was worth 30 Slurpees to me. Since that time, I have been careful when spending money to determine whether the money would be better spent elsewhere.

When I was in college, I had a deal with my parents: If I got scholarships to cover 100 percent of tuition and room and board, they'd pay for a credit card bill in full for living and entertainment expenses so I didn't have to have a job and could concentrate on extracurricular activities and internships. (This all happened.) However, my dad wanted to make sure I *understood* what I was spending money on, so he would mail me the credit card statement each month after he paid it. He would highlight lines and make comments about what the various charges were for: "Fun. Fun. Clothes. Fun. Clothes. Party. Beer. Books. Paid for courtesy of dear old Dad." While I appreciated him paying, it brought attention to where I was

spending money frivolously, even though it wasn't mine and didn't *hurt* my bottom line to spend it. He made me realize what *he* was paying for, instead of leaving me blind and in the dark about it. I still look at my statements every month and itemize by category, and try to reduce the amount of "Clothes, Fun, Beer,…" and prioritize more important things.

In our survey, we asked, "What do you wish you would have been taught about money?" Here is what our respondents had to say:

- Save as early as you can and keep it up
- Have an emergency fund
- Give 10 percent to charity and save 10 percent first before spending a dime
- Start your retirement fund early
- Learn to negotiate salary
- Budgeting
- Investing
- Money doesn't solve all of your problems
- Debt and credit
- It's okay to talk about money

C'est La Vie!

Be diligent with your work. Household chores are a great place to start teaching your young children to develop good work habits and a strong work ethic. The 2010 Charles Schwab Survey seems to agree too, revealing the strong correlation between childhood chores and financial independence in adulthood. Those children that had four or more regular chores were the most financially responsible. Simple tasks like folding laundry, picking up around the house, gardening, and setting and clearing the table are all great ways to have your child help.

I remember my daughter playing in the room with me while I was folding laundry. It was a game for her to match the socks, and she really enjoyed helping me. For a toddler, that's building confidence in her abilities to help around the house. Other easy chores for children, beginning at toddlerhood, include feeding their pet(s), setting the napkins on the table

for dinner, picking up their toys, watering plants, wiping off the table after dinner and putting their clean clothes back in their dresser drawers. As they get a little older, they may feel like it's more of a chore (hence the phrase, "doing chores"), but it still needs to get done. It can be hard to cut back on a housekeeper, but you'll save money *and* teach your children about responsibility and work ethic.

Exposure, exposure, exposure. Teach your child how to do their own laundry, even if you have hired help. There is just something really sad about an adult who can't wash their own clothes. Having enough resources to be able to pay someone else to help with your housework, yard work and errands is wonderful, but a child needs to understand two things: One, the person helping your family isn't just volunteering. They're spending their time helping you and you are paying them—it's called work. Having help costs money. Second, they may need to do the things that you're paying someone to do and they need that exposure before college. It's great that someone cleans your house, but your child is going to have to clean their own house someday. He or she needs to know how, that it costs money and that it is not beneath them.

I really wish they still taught Home Economics (aka Family and Consumer Sciences) in school. Kids learned how to cook for themselves, clean their house, hygiene, family resource management, consumerism and other vocational skills. I would love to see this back in school. I had a father who was pretty handy, so I learned how to do quite a few things around the house. I've also volunteered at Habitat for Humanity, which really strengthened my knowledge of my home. I love that I've had contractors come to my house and try to pull one over on me…education is powerful. Responsibility in daily life plays into being more financially responsible.

My daughter actually started looking forward to feeding our dog Winston and got upset if I forgot and did it myself. She assumed the responsibility of feeding him and started to take pride in taking care of

"her" dog. In feeding him, they began bonding more and he started looking to her as more of a "master" than as the other person that lived with us that liked to dress him up. This one task had the ripple effect of pride, ownership and responsibility in my daughter, as well as loyalty and companionship with our dog.

Just imagine all the other lessons that can come out of our day-to-day activities in which we involve our children! One other lesson we must keep in the forefront of our minds is *patience* on our part. Being a self-diagnosed Type-A personality, I like things clean. The dog food may not always make it cleanly into the dog bowl, the folded clothes may not look folded once they've made their way into my daughter's dresser drawers and water in plants outside may mean a change of clothes, but it still is best for your child to learn to take on these responsibilities. Over time, they do get better, and practicing teaches yet another nugget of wisdom: We don't always get it right the first time, and practice and patience are needed in life. Just be aware not to let out any frustrations with your kids and not to punish or demean them for being imperfect. You'd be doing much more harm to your child. So what if the dog food gets on the floor? So what if they get a little wet watering the plants? Shrug it off and keep a smile on your face to show how *proud* of them you are. A high-five or a "thank you for helping" or "I'm so proud of you" is a nice way to end the chore. Positive affirmation will encourage future positive behavior.

Part of life is doing things you don't always want to do. Wow, how many parents of teenagers have said that to their kids? "Honey, that's just life!" We may even get creative and start using the French version of the saying and spout out, *"C'est la vie!"* Teach this lesson along the way and you won't hear yourself using that phrase daily when they call you complaining in college that they "have" to do laundry or moaning about having to cook for themselves. You want them to come visit you on the weekend to see you, not just to drop off laundry. Take it a step farther and remind them

that they may graduate from school and end up doing a JOB that they don't particularly like doing all the time. "Honey, that's just life." And then there are those times they may work for little or no pay, but it was a good career move. There may be a great internship opportunity without pay. It's doing things that need to be done not just because we got some immediate reward.

Beware of entitlement. It runs long and deep. You can spot it easily. I am, therefore I deserve_____. Most entitlement issues are learned. It is often such an internal struggle for most parents. We want to provide for our children the best we can and take care of their needs. Most of us want to provide them with a better life than we've had. At what point do we let them in on the big secret—that you can't always get what you want? For parents, part of it is imagining the person whose diaper you changed umpteen times growing up. It is frightening. You may also fear losing the innocence of your child. You're the caretaker, and all they should think about is imaginative play and learning their ABCs. Now, they get to learn about money and responsibility.

Tell your kids stories of what your first job was like or how you made money raking the neighbor's leaves in the fall. They'll love learning more about you, but also, these stories will show them how hard you've worked for the things your family has. An employee, when asked to stay and work until 6 p.m., won't pout to his Facebook friends about it if he's heard his parents talk about working late sometimes—and get fired for it when his boss reads the post. Trust me, having a dad that worked an occasional Saturday made it a lot more bearable when I had to do it for the first time. I was just following in my father's footsteps. It's just part of working—you have to do things sometimes that you don't like, but it's a job and you do it anyway.

Unfortunately today, many children are raised with entitlement issues. I truly don't think as a parent that's our intention, but rather the outcome

of how we dealt with money in the family. As parents, we don't want our children to feel discomfort. Discomfort could be not having the toy or video game that the other kids have, having to do chores around the house or the yard, having to get a part-time job to help with household expenses or not being part of a social group. From an early age, we see kids trying to keep up with social trends. In the 80s, I remember all the crazy fad wardrobes that must have driven our parents crazy. I can only imagine my daughter coming to me to buy plastic neon pants. The jelly shoes are already back.

There always have been and always will be fads. It's the role of marketing and consumerism to come up with the next big thing that we can't live without. We can't pin the blame on the kids, either. I've seen people pay thousands of dollars on flat screen televisions when they didn't have the equivalent amount in their savings account but they just *had* to have that television for whatever reason (excuse) they told themselves and charged it. I'll admit, we finally got our flat screen television, but only after our other one died, and it had lasted ten years. Guess what? We paid quite a bit less than those that rushed out and bought them when they first came out. Practice patience with yourself and your children will learn from you.

We'd rather give our children what they want so they don't feel discomfort, which helps us not feel discomfort. Or, we feel that we need something to feel comfort ourselves. If your child doesn't learn to tolerate discomfort, he's going to be a very frustrated adolescent and adult, according to behavioral therapist Dr. James Lehman. We've had the trophy generation where you didn't get a trophy for winning; you just had to show up to get one. That's not the real world. You see children graduating from college without ever having to lift a finger around the house, without having to ever pay for anything, and they expect to have a 1,500 square-foot apartment, a flat screen television, full cable package, cell phone with unlimited texting, a new car, and the list goes on. Could it get worse? Yes, because all

the credit card companies welcomed them to college with applications for credit cards that they gladly accepted. According to U.S. Citizens for Fair Credit Card Terms, Inc., an organization devoted to educating consumers about credit cards, credit card companies spend $6 billion each year mailing credit card solicitations. Your up-and-coming adult now has credit card bills mounting and the avalanche starts. I've had people in their early 20s come into my office and ask about bankruptcy. That should never happen. Teach your child about credit. This book will help you do that.

For those of you reading this that have ever felt you deserved a certain lifestyle or you have certain minimum standards for your lifestyle or ever felt like you may just need certain things to be happy, I need to talk with you a bit, so please take what I'm about to say to heart. I really think it's wonderful that we have gotten to a place in history where we have so many inventions, so many options and opportunities. In this regard, we are truly blessed. If parents always provided for you, I will not question one bit their love for you. If things happen to fall in your lap, or if you truly feel that someone will always be there to catch you if you fall, that's wonderful to have a strong sense of community and relationships. There is a time when you must be able to stand on your own two feet. For many, the time is when they graduate from high school. Others can wait until college or post-graduate education to experience this. The older you are when you are finally on your own, the longer you've been under someone else's wing. You may determine that this was a good thing since it allowed you to get your education, have a place to live or live it up in your 20s or 30s. There can be a downside to this. The more we're set in our ways with a certain lifestyle, the harder it is to "downgrade" when we're on our own. You're set to live in a certain part of town or have a certain car, tech toys, furnishings or friendships. Maybe all the people in that community go to a certain country club and you feel you need to join in order to fit in, but you don't have the money to. I've seen people whose rent or mortgage consumed 50 percent or more of their income, and they

were going deeper into debt every month because after all of their money went into their home, they didn't have much left for the car payment, food and healthcare. If all of your friends call you on a $500 phone, you feel you need that phone in order to communicate. Maybe you feel you need to send your child to a certain school, so you live in an area way beyond your means, or that you need to send your kids to a certain private school because you went there or all of your friends' kids are there. With true friends, you can be honest with them and say that you're sorry you can't join them, but that just doesn't fit with your plans. I have been in your shoes and do understand.

I remember being invited to a friend's beach house one summer with a group of my girlfriends, but I was just starting my career and couldn't afford the cost of the trip. I hated not going. I was afraid I'd miss out on the memories, the camaraderie and the fun. After much deliberation, I told them I just couldn't afford to go. Of course, I got the pressure. "Of course you can go, just put it on your credit card and pay it off over time…it will be so much fun!" The pressure was tough, but I stood my ground and said I really wanted to go, thanked them for including me, but it just wasn't in my budget and I wasn't willing to take on huge interest charges by carrying that credit card debt. They went without me and I'm sure had fun. I'm still happy about the decision I made and the people that were really my friends are still my friends today. I'm older now and have done a good job of saving and budgeting and have taken some fun girls' trips, but only when I could afford them.

The same process goes with your peers that all live in the hottest apartment or who are going off on the ski trip. You have to be honest with yourself, and if you can't pay for it, don't do it. There is no shame in building your career, a new life for yourself after a divorce or just starting off later in life. You must take the time to budget, analyze your money and determine whether it's a good decision for you at the time. You'll feel much better

living below your means for a while to save up so that you can actually afford what you want or need to do.

Maybe that means renting a smaller apartment for a couple of years so that you can put that 20-percent down payment on a house. Two years of a life is just a blink. It may mean driving your car a while longer than you would have liked and putting off the new one until you could either pay cash for it or put some money down to make the payments more affordable. Life always, always happens when you least expect it, so living a lifestyle you can afford, even if you lost a job for a period of time or had a big financial emergency, is one of the best financial lessons I can share with you. I could tell hundreds of stories about life happening and savings getting wiped out. You don't want to be one of those stories. Don't replace long-term stability for short-term gratification.

Beware never to bring up money in arguments or power struggles. Using money with strings attached is going down the wrong path. You don't want your child to think you can be bought, or else she'll only behave if given monetary rewards. You see the adult version of these kids and it's still apparent in their lives. They reward themselves with purchases. *If I do this, I'll reward myself by buying that,* they think. Rewards become more frequent, and the serious cases end up with mounting credit card debt or little money left in savings. They're not living any differently than their parents did. Their friends all got the hot phone, a flat screen TV, an SUV. "That's not fair," they protested. I kid you not. I've heard actual adults say those words. Well, at least they didn't have a "throw down."

The Coconut Monkey

When you go on vacation, set aside an amount of money or vacation allowance for each child. Let the child know the amount before the trip starts. If they want to blow the entire amount the first day, talk them through how that's the end of their money. If they want to go ahead, let them. They'll either be glad they did or feel a little upset. Either way, a good lesson was taught in saving and spending. As a parent, this allows you to budget for the expenses and not have to have an argument at every store. You gave them the ability to make decisions.

I remember going on vacation to Cancun, Mexico, when I was a preteen. It was near the end of our trip and I spotted a coconut carved into a monkey. Ironically, it was a coconut monkey safe and had a coin slot carved into the chest. I have no idea what my parents spent on that thing, but I just *had* to have that coconut monkey. My purpose in telling this story

is not that the coconut monkey made the trip memorable. I actually was going through a box my mother gave me that was full of random childhood trinkets. Inside that box was the coconut monkey. I thought about passing it off as a horrible white elephant party gift, but it was truly too hideous for even a white elephant party. I threw it in the trash. How it made it in a box in my parents' attic for 25 years is beyond me, but my point is this: Give your child a set vacation allowance, even a very small amount for them to buy something to remember the trip. If they end up bringing home a coconut monkey, so be it, but your vacation allowance limits the *stuff* that comes home with you and possibly limits the stuff in the attic.

Saving, Spending and Giving

Plant the Saving Seed

Saving is delayed spending. The habit of saving starting at age 4 or 5 will give your child a *huge* leg up in the world of financial management. Forgoing today's "wants" for tomorrows "needs or wants" is something that many adults struggle with. If it was part of life from the very beginning, I don't think we'd have such a hard time with it as adults. Start the habit early. The savings and matching strategy is great when the kids get older and have bigger-ticket items they want. The cell phone they want may cost $300, but you may agree to match their savings so that they only need to save $150 to get it. You're showing your kids that things in life aren't free and that you need to set aside money to get what you want.

The same concept can be used for a car, preferably used if it's their first. I remember the first car I bought. I was 18 years old. It was a black Mitsubishi Eclipse. I was paying a portion from money I'd saved up over the years working odd and summer jobs, and my dad was pitching in the rest. Since I needed to limit what I spent on the car, I opted out of electric windows, electric locks and the automatic transmission. I had never driven a stick shift in my life, but that was all I could afford. We bought the car and my father proceeded to get into the passenger seat...after all, this was *my* car! Gulp. The car dealership was just off the highway and we needed to get on it to get home in five o'clock traffic in Dallas, Texas. I learned to drive stick shift in about five minutes! My father acted very calm, but as a parent now, I'm sure he was holding his breath the whole time and probably sweating profusely. I remember his saying, "Ashley, if you're going to learn stick, well, this is the time to do it. After all it's your car." We got home safely that day. I came back with more than a new car: I learned how to buy the car, I learned the cost of all the extras that add to the price of buying a vehicle and I had an overwhelming sense of accomplishment. I knew what it took for me to own that car. It cost countless hours of hard work and the willpower to save the money I earned. I was so fortunate that my family helped pay for the car, and for that I am truly grateful. I took so much better care of that car knowing what it took to bring it home. We often value things more when we've had to work for them.

Spending Seeds

Spending is the opposite of earning. This is money that your child can use to buy things they need. As parents, model this behavior for your children. Give them examples of how you spend money, like at the grocery store or putting gas in your car. With younger children, certain concepts just don't make sense to them, so keep any financial lessons simple and easy for them to understand. The Spending Jar can be used if your child really wants to order take-out somewhere or go to a fun restaurant. Obviously, they won't be picking up the entire tab with their Spending Jar, but having them contribute something, anything, is teaching them to pitch in for things they want. Explaining that money doesn't grow on trees will only elicit a smug, "No, Mommy, *leaves* grow on trees." But having money come out of their jar to eat out may really make them pause and question whether it's worth spending.

If times are tough, see what you can do as a family to make the gloomy situation become a positive for your family. Maybe you can't go out to eat as often, so plan family time at home cooking together. Maybe you can't afford a vacation this year, so get creative with a *"stay*-cation." Get the family involved on all the fun activities you can do in your own town, your own community. There is always a positive and a negative way to see any circumstance. You'll be amazed at how much joy can come from seeing the glass half-full and showing your kids how to enjoy life in both the lean and plentiful times.

There was a time when I was just out of school and wanted to get some Christmas presents for some of my friends. I was on a tight budget but wanted to get them something meaningful. I found some great cookie cutters at a store warehouse sale for $2.50 a box. I kicked in my creativity and picked up a few boxes for gifts. My presentation was the box full of cookie cutters with my grandmother's delicious cookie cutter recipe from 1976, along with a short paragraph about the recipe's legacy. They *loved* the sentimental gift, and they continue to make those cookies for their families. A simple gift turned out to be an enduring tradition, and all for less than a few bucks. Get your kids involved in the creativity and you will have hit the ball out of the park.

Sharing And Caring

Giving can come in many forms. We introduce the concept of giving with sharing. With sharing, you're giving up control of what you have for a period of time so that someone else can use it. Giving it means letting that person have it for good. You can give your time, talent and treasure (money). Encourage all three forms. Time can be in spending time with family members or relatives, volunteering at a local organization or even at school. Children need to understand the concept of giving back, and volunteering is a wonderful, inexpensive way to do that. Giving their talent could be through painting a mural for a local center, tutoring other children, singing in a choir. If your child likes to cook, he or she could cook meals and then deliver them to the local food bank or bake cookies for the local nursing home. Get to know what your child does well and what she enjoys and encourage her to do that for the good of your community.

Your child's talents can also be great ways to earn extra money for that Spending or Savings Jar. I know a family in which the daughter loves horseback riding and wanted to take lessons every week. Well, that can get costly. A great solution was that she was able to help out at the stables to earn the money to pay for her weekly lessons. She learned even more about horses by taking care of them and helping the equestrian center and, at the same time, she could continue to pursue her passion of riding horses.

Maybe your child loves soccer. He or she may be able to teach younger children soccer lessons and earn some extra cash while enjoying his or her passion for soccer. Bake sales, tutoring, lawn services and babysitting can be great ways to earn extra income. Adults can also find ways to use their talents, such as bartering with your athletic club for free membership in exchange for teaching a class.

Giving money can be the most difficult for some people. Remember that we started out with the "That's Mine" syndrome. Having earned money and then not being able to use it for yourself can be hard, which is why it's important to talk with your child about causes or organizations that are near and dear to them. If your child's favorite thing to do every night is reading books, talk to your child about the fact that there are many children who can't buy books because they can't afford them. You and your child could give away the books he or she no longer reads or buy gently used books with money in the Giving Jar and donate them to children's literacy groups or through a program at your local library. Another idea would be buying plants to brighten up the landscape at a school or senior center. If you have a pet lover, donating to the SPCA or your family pet's local rescue association may be a good fit. They can immediately see the impact of providing food and shelter to those furry friends of ours that give us so much in return. Texas A&M University College of Veterinary Medicine and Biomedical Sciences was established in 1916. Their Mission states, "We, the faculty and staff of the College of Veterinary Medicine &

Biomedical Sciences, are a community of scholars committed to: Caring about animals and people; curing and preventing animal disease; creating new knowledge, new therapies, and new learning opportunities; and communicating with students, veterinarians, scientists, and the public." Being an Aggie and an animal lover, this may fit with my desires to donate both to my alma mater as well as supporting a cause I'm passionate about. You may want to research ways to give back to an organization that you feel a connection with to see what research projects they're involved in and donate there. Donating to an institution of higher learning is another great opportunity to give back.

Maybe you had a family member who was diagnosed with a disease such as heart disease or cancer. Making a gift to the American Heart Association or American Cancer Society is meaningful to them, and the gift can be specifically made in that family member's honor. Just make sure to let your child decide where to give and support them in the process, whether it be through shopping for the materials, driving them to the donation center or putting a check in the mail for them.

Donating money to a religious organization may be most suited for your family. You can usually specify which cause or project the money can be allocated for or you can also donate to the organization and have them use the funds at their discretion. Whichever route you go, giving to others is an important lesson for us all.

Growing Your Seeds

There is one last category that will come into play when your child is a little older: investing. An investment is money set aside with the goal of appreciation (growth) or income. This is money saved that we set aside for a later use (long-term) that requires careful consideration. In order to save for your children's college, you may invest in a college savings plan.

When your child is old enough, start discussing different types of investments. A good place to start is with your own portfolio. Talk about your retirement plan and how it works. Show them how you contribute to the account and how you chose the investments. Teach them the definition of a stock, mutual fund and bond. Giving them these general concepts further enhances their exposure to money and how it's used, how it grows and its role in our society.

Your home may be one of the largest assets you own. Talk with your child about buying a home, putting money down to buy it, the long-term nature of the investment and what it costs to run your home and pay the mortgage every month. Exposing your child to your investments adds relevance and gives your child some basic knowledge about what it means to be an adult with adult responsibilities and commitments. If they're a teenager when you buy your next car, take them with you. They'll need to buy one someday. Show them what it's like to go to the various car lots, how to determine your budget and how you're going to pay. I was 18 when I got my first car. I remember sitting with my father in the car salesman's office negotiating the sale.

Teach your child, and yourself, the Rule of 72. The Rule of 72 is a simple way to understand compound interest. In order to see how long it would take your money to double, divide 72 by the interest rate. For example, if you earn an 8-percent rate of return, it would take (72 ÷ 8) 9 years for your money to double. The actual number of years is 9.01, but the Rule of 72 gets it close enough.

Maybe you're only earning 2 percent on your money. That would take (72 ÷ 2) 36 years for your money to double! Now, take this example a bit farther. Let's say you calculate how much the future cost of your child's education would be. Let's assume we have a crystal ball and we know exactly what it's going to cost. If you only earn 2 percent versus 8 percent, it's going to take quite a bit more savings to reach that goal.

An important concept in money management is that money is neutral; it's neither good nor bad. It has the potential to be both, but money in and of itself is not good or bad. I've known people who thought having money was a bad thing because it meant greed or extreme frugality. Many others thought money was good because it gave them the ability to get their wants met or it allowed them to establish savings. It's how we treat money and use it in our lives that makes it either good or bad. The question to ask yourself is whether you are a good steward of your money or not. Remember, it's not what you told your children about money that's important; it's how you lived with your money and taught them by being a good example. As parents, we need to show our children how to be good savers, spenders and givers.

Time to Grow

Ilook at my daughter with such awe. I go from *"Did you really live inside my belly?"* to *"I can't believe you're already so grown up."* As a parent, on some level I want her to remain naive to some parts of life. She's not yet had a friend turn on her. She's yet to have a boy break her heart. The older we get, the more of life we've experienced. We've lived through friends and relatives passing away, we've seen infidelities in relationships and we've experienced betrayals. We've seen markets up 50 percent and down 50 percent, businesses succeed and fail. As I'm writing this book, 1 out of every 10 adults is out of a job. There are real hardships and tough realities to face in life, and as parents or guardians we want to shelter our children as long as we can. We have this protective instinct and want to shield them from all the disappointments, falls and hurts in life. The dilemma is that whether we like it or not, it's either going to be us to lead them or someone else. Our children are going to grow up, and it is our

responsibility to make every effort to love, support, guide, educate and care for them. One day, sooner than we may like, our children will become adults. They will have the responsibility to make financial decisions daily, to pay bills, save for their life goals, start a career and eventually lead their own families. Imagine future generations of people living within their means, saving for their goals, managing debt responsibly and feeling free to talk about money in their homes and communities.

These children are our future leaders, doctors, business managers and teachers. While they're still under your wing you have the opportunity and ability to help shape their views and values about money. Dr. Klontz suggests that "our behaviors around money are influencing the next generation and the degree to which we are conscious and deliberately choose these behaviors is the degree to which they will be the same."

Think about what you're teaching them already and what needs to change. How well are you communicating with your child in a way they can understand? In our survey, one parent admitted she did everything wrong when it came to money. She said her children learned to save and to be thrifty after seeing her and her husband forced to downsize, climb out of debt and have no money left in savings or retirement. Some of the stories had such *unfortunate irony*. There was the mother who spent a fortune repeatedly redecorating her house and now is soon to be homeless. Proverbs 14:1 says, "A wise woman builds her home, but a foolish woman tears it down with her own hands."

There are things in life beyond our control, but many of our problems are ones we created for ourselves. When will be your time to change? I understand how difficult change is. In every person's life, we have to face some pretty major truths, either about ourselves or the way the world works or just about life. As we age, we truly see more of the world, both the good and the bad.

I encourage parents and mentors to point out change that is occurring all around them. The next time the seasons change, take the time to explore what's happening and talk about it with your kids. This is a great opportunity to open up the dialogue about change. As your children grow, their bodies change, their interests change and so does the world around them. Point out the beauty and energy that springs from change because change is just part of life. Where do we need to change? What about our financial lives doesn't fit with what we find most important, what we value? What from our past have we not come to terms with, and what emotional or financial baggage are we carrying? Once we're really honest with ourselves, the truth becomes clear. It's like the fog has finally lifted and we're faced with a decision. Are we going to keep hanging onto normalcy even if it's not healthy for us? Or are we going to finally decide to take the weight off, prune the tree and courageously blaze a new path? The image of a caterpillar transforming into a butterfly comes to mind. What I found is that I had been crawling along, looking up at what was above me, and yearning to fly. It wasn't until I got out of my shell that I realized I had wings.

The big question is whether we're going to change, maybe even adapt, or better yet, to grow. Speaking from experience, change can be very difficult, but I've found that personal improvement is the very best investment you can ever make. Like forming any new habit, there's a period of change and with that is discomfort. It may be difficult for a while not to go shopping if that was a habit of yours. Make it a daily effort, and if you ever get off course—which you probably will since you're only human—start back up the next day. Having an accountability partner you check in with will increase your chances of success.

This book doesn't give one formula for success like many have promised in the past. It took personal time, energy and money for me to write this book, and I feel you deserve the truth. I want to equip you with tools you can use to increase the probability for successfully planting healthy seeds

and creating strong roots for your family tree. If you can change within and start to live life with your values and be true to yourself, then truth and authenticity will pervade all parts of your life. Tracy Chapman has a wonderful song called *"Change."* The lyrics talk about chain reactions from our actions and challenge us to think about how far we'll let things go before we're ready to change. *"How bad, how good does it need to get? How many losses? How much regret? What chain reaction would cause an effect? Makes you turn around, makes you try to explain, makes you forgive and forget, makes you change."*

The seeds that were planted in you affect who you are today and what you are planting in your children. According to *National Geographic News*, the world's oldest living tree can be found in Sweden, at the ripe age of 9,550 years old (Owen). Leif Kullman, professor of ecology and environmental science at Umea University in Sweden, told *National Geographic* that the tree's longevity is due to its ability to clone itself. The stems have a lifespan of 600 years "but as soon as a stem dies, a new one emerges from the same root stock." The tree has survived for over nine thousand years due to its strong root system.

Growing up, my father used to read *The Giving Tree* by Shel Silverstein (Silverstein), in the evening before bed time. When my daughter was born, I perused the aisles of the book store, choosing books for her that had meant something to me as a child, hoping to bring back some fond memories for me and begin new ones for her. I picked up a copy of *The Giving Tree* off the shelf and toted it home with my other nostalgic finds. That evening, I sat down in my favorite reading chair, nestled her on my lap and began to read that same story that I remembered so fondly from my youth. As I read through the book, my heart sank. I realized how sad the story was. The story begins with the boy playing games with the tree, eating her apples and resting in her shade. As the boy grew up, he took all of her apples to sell, cut down all her branches to build a house and sawed off her trunk to create a boat to run away from the problems in his life. He left nothing

more than a stump, on which he later returned to sit. In closing the book, I was frustrated with the boy and the tree. Could the boy not get a job and save up money for a house instead of taking everything from the tree? When life was too hard for him, could he not have sought guidance instead of cutting down the tree and sailing away? The tree let the boy take everything she had simply because she loved him.

It takes effort to plant healthy seeds. It takes commitment to nurture those seeds to maturity. Long term, if the *Giving Tree* said "no" to the boy, and helped him work through the changes in his life, she would have been able to love and influence many more children through the years as well as help the boy grow strong roots within himself. Think big and be greater than you are now. Plant saving seeds in your family and grow a financially healthy family tree today.

> *A truly good book teaches me better than to read it.*
> *I must soon lay it down, and commence living on its hint.*
> *What I began by reading, I must finish by acting.*

Henry David Thoreau

315914 DOFU 6/2011

Appendix

COVER ILLUSTRATOR

ROBERT FORSBACH

WORKS CITED

Affairs, United States Department of Veterans. "Born of Contoversy: The GI Bill of Rights." 2009.

Awareness, Council for Disability. "The 2010 Council for Disability Awareness Long Term Disability Claims Review." 2010.

Begley, Sharon. Train Your Mind, Change Your Brain: How a New Science Reveals Our Extraordinary Potention to Transform Ourselves. Ballantine Books, 2007.

Blayney, Eleanor. Women's Worth: Finding Your Financial Confidence. First. Direction$ LLC, 2010.

Bright, Catherine. Attorney-Board Certified Estate Planning Ashley Parks. 6 April 2011.

Bureau, US Census. "Statistical Abstract of the United States 2011." 2008.

Chapman, Dr. Gary. The 5 Love Languages: The Secret to Love That Lasts. 1992: Northfield Publishing, n.d.

Commission, Federal Trade. Federal Trade Commission. 2011. 30 June 2011 <www.ftc.gov/bcp/edu/microsites/freereports/idex.shtml>.

Getz, David. "Men's and Women's Earnings for States and Metropolitan Statistical AreasL 2009. U.S. Census Bureau, ACSBT/09-3." (2010).

Hallowell, Dr. Edward. Crazy Busy: Overstretched, Overbooked, and About to Snap! Strategies for Handling Your Fast-Paced Life. Ballantine Books, 2007.

Klontz, Drs. Brad and Ted. Mind over Money: Overcoming the Money Disorders that Threaten Our Financial Health. New York: Crown Business, 2009.

Kontz, Dr. Ted. Interview. Ashley Parks. 29 July 2011.

Labor, US Department of. "Quick Stats on Women Workers, 2009." 2009.

LaMorgese, Brad. Attorney-Board Certified Family Law Ashley Parks. 13 April 2011.

Lehrer, Jonah. "DON'T: The Secret of Self-Control." The New Yorker (2009).

Losier, Michael. Law of Attraction: The Science of Attracting More of What You Want and Less of What You Don't. Grand Central Publishing, 2004.

McCloud, Carol. <u>Have You Filled a Bucket Today: A Guide to Daily Happiness for Kids.</u> Ferne Press, 2006.

McGarrahan, Dr. Andrew. <u>Clinical Psychologist</u> Ashley Parks. 21 October 2010.

Mehrabian, Dr. Albert. "Silent Messages." 1981.

Mischel, Walter, Yuichi Shoda and Monica Rodriguez. "Delay of Gratification In Children." <u>Science</u> 26 May 1989.

Muriel, James and Dorothy Jongeward. <u>Born to Win: Transactional Analysis with Gestalt Experiments.</u> Addison-Wesley Publishing Company, Inc., 1971.

Owen, James. "Oldest Living Tree Found in Sweden." <u>National Geographic</u> (2008).

Pediatrics, American Academy of. "Children Who Prosper in Unfavorable Environments: The Relationship to Social Capital." <u>Journal of the American Academy of Pediatrics, Volume 101, No.1</u> (1998): 12-18.

Perry, Lisa. <u>Founder of The Well Blended Family</u> Ashley Parks. 7 July 2011.

Planning, FDIC Division of Research and Strategic. "The First Fifty Years: A History of the FDIC 1933-1983." 1984.

Rogers, Carl. <u>On Becoming A Person.</u> Houghton Mifflin, 1961.

Schwab, Charles. "Charles Schwab 2010 Families & Money Survey: Insights into Money Attitudes, Behaviors and Concerns of The Sandwich Generation (Americans with Young Adult Children, Ages 23-28, and Living Parents)." 2010.

Shrestha, Laura B. "Life Expectancy in the United States, CRS Report for Congress." 2006.

Silverstein, Shel. The Giving Tree. Harper & Row, 1964.

Statistics, Bureau of Labor. "Household Data Not Seasonally Adjusted. Employed Persons by occupation, sex, and age." (2011).

Statistics, US Bureau of Labor. "U.S. Bureau of Labor Statistics, Consumer Expenditure Survey, and U.S. Census Bureau, Statistical Abstract of the United States." n.d.

SyberVision Systems. The Neuropsychology of Self-Discipline. Sybervision Systems, 2002.

Sykes, Charles J. Dumbing Down Our Kids: Why American Children Feel Good About Themselves But Can't Read, Write, or Add. St. Martin's Griffin, 1996.

Thomas Stanley, Ph.D. and William Danko, Ph.D. The Millionaire Next Door. Longstreet Press, Inc., 1996.

Winterman, Denise. "What would a real life Barbie look like?" BBC News Magazine (2009).

Wyly, Sam. 1,000 Dollars & An Idea: Entrepreneur to Billionaire. New York: Newmarket Press, 2009.